DEVELOPMENT FINANCING AND CHANGES IN CIRCUMSTANCES

A PUBLICATION OF THE GRADUATE INSTITUTE OF INTERNATIONAL STUDIES, GENEVA

Also published in this series:

The United States and the Politicization of the World Bank
Bartram S. Brown

Trade Negotiations in the OECD
David J. Blair

World Financial Markets after 1992
Hans Genberg and Alexander K. Swoboda

Succession Between International Organisations
Patrick R. Myers

Ten Years of Turbulence: The Chinese Cultural Revolution
Barbara Barnouin and Yu Changgen

The Islamic Movement in Egypt: Perceptions of International Relations 1967–81
Walid M. Abdelnasser

Namibia and Southern Africa: Regional Dynamics of Decolonization 1945–90
Ronald Dreyer

The International Organization of Hunger
Peter Uvin

Citizenship East and West
Edited by André Liebich and Daniel Warner
with Jasna Dragović

Introduction to the Law of Treaties
Paul Reuter

The Imperiled Red Cross and the Palestine-Eretz-Yisrael Conflict 1945–1952
Dominique-D. Junod

Ideology and Economic Reform Under Deng Xiaoping, 1978–1993
Wei-Wei Zhang

Chinese Foreign Policy During the Cultural Revolution
Barbara Barnouin and Yu Changgen

Modern Aspects of the Laws of Naval Warfare and Maritime Neutrality
George P. Politakis

DEVELOPMENT FINANCING AND CHANGES IN CIRCUMSTANCES

The Case for Adaptation Clauses

Bolívar Moura Rocha

KEGAN PAUL INTERNATIONAL
London and New York

First published in 1999 by
Kegan Paul International
UK: P.O. Box 256, London WC1B 3SW, England
Tel: (0171) 580 5511 Fax: (0171) 436 0899
E-mail: books@keganpau.demon.co.uk
Internet: http://www.demon.co.uk/keganpaul/
USA: 562 West 113th Street, New York, NY 10025, USA
Tel: (212) 666 1000 Fax: (212) 316 3100

Distributed by

John Wiley & Sons Ltd
Southern Cross Trading Estate
1 Oldlands Way, Bognor Regis
West Sussex, PO22 9SA, England
Tel: (01243) 779 777 Fax: (01243) 820 250

Columbia University Press
562 West 113th Street
New York, NY 10025, USA
Tel: (212) 666 1000 Fax: (212) 316 3100

Set in 10 on 12 pt Palatino
by Intype London Ltd
Printed in Great Britain

British Library Cataloguing in Publication Data
Rocha, Bolívar Moura
 Development financing and changes in circumstances: the case for adaptation
 clauses. – (A publication of the Graduate Institute of International Studies,
 Geneva)
 1. Debt relief – Developing countries 2. Loans, Foreign – Developing
 countries 3. Clauses (Law)
 I. Title II. Graduate Institute of International Studies
 336.3'435'091724

 ISBN 0–7103–0590–7

Library of Congress Cataloging-in-Publication Data
Moura Rocha, Bolívar, 1964–
 Development financing and changes in circumstances: the case for adaptation
 clauses/Bolívar Moura Rocha.
   p. cm. — (A publication of the Graduate Institute of International
 Studies, Geneva)
 Includes bibliographical references.
 ISBN 0–7103–0590–7
 1. Loans, Foreign – Law and legislation. 2. Debts, External—Law and
 legislator. 3. International finance—Law and legislation. 4. Loans,
 Foreign—Developing countries. 5. Debts, External—Developing countries.
 I. Title. II. Series: Publications de l'Institut universitaire de hautes études
 internationales, Genève.
 K4450.M68 1998
 341.7'6115—dc21   97–50134
                                                                        CIP

To Moura and Ibelza

CONTENTS

vii

CONTENTS

ABBREVIATIONS

ADB	Asian Development Bank
AfDB	African Development Bank
CFR	(US) Code of Federal Regulations
EBRD	European Bank for Reconstruction and Development
FDIC	(US) Federal Deposit Insurance Corporation
FT	FINANCIAL TIMES
ICJ	International Court of Justice
ICLQ	INTERNATIONAL AND COMPARATIVE LAW QUARTERLY
IFLR	INTERNATIONAL FINANCIAL LAW REVIEW
ILM	INTERNATIONAL LEGAL MATERIALS
IBRD	International Bank for Reconstruction and Development
ICSID	International Center for the Settlement of Investment Disputes
IDB	Inter-American Development Bank
IMF	International Monetary Fund
IOSCO	International Organization of Securities Commissions
LDC	Less developed country
LIBOR	London Inter-Bank Offered (Interest) Rate
MIGA	Multilateral Investments Guarantee Agency
OJ	OFFICIAL JOURNAL OF THE EUROPEAN COMMUNITIES
OCC	(US) Office of the Comptroller of the Currency
PCIJ	Permanent Court of International Justice
RCADI	COLLECTED COURSES OF THE HAGUE ACADEMY OF INTERNATIONAL LAW

ABBREVIATIONS

TIAS	(United States) Treaties and Other International Acts Series
UNCTAD	United Nations Conference on Trade and Development
UNTS	United Nations Treaty Series

TABLE OF CASES

FOREWORD

In the academic year 1986–1987, my first at the Graduate Institute of International Studies, I enrolled at Professor Stuart Robinson's seminar on *droit financier et monétaire international*, and undertook to present a seminar paper on the topic of *sovereign lending*. My attention was caught by one particular aspect of the literature describing the floating interest rate loan agreements which constituted the main instrument for development financing throughout the 1970s and early 1980s. It was the fact that loan documentation would typically provide for protection to lenders against changes in circumstances, while no symmetrical treatment was granted to borrowers. The 'unfair' – to the mind of a law school graduate recently arrived from Brazil – nature of this contractual imbalance was demonstrated, I believed, by the fact that it was precisely sudden and dramatic changes in circumstances that prompted the so-called developing country debt crisis of the 1980s.

While I later came to have a better understanding of the reasons underlying that apparent bias of loan agreements to which developing country borrowers were parties, one question remained in my mind as worthy of closer analysis, namely that regarding the potential benefits of having documentation evidencing developing country indebtedness provide for contractual relief for borrowers in case of adverse changes in circumstances. Under the ever wise advice and guidance of Professor Stuart Robinson, I decided to pursue that issue as the core question addressed in my doctoral dissertation. In that endeavor, the professional activities I undertook in the meantime threw practical light on the analysis: I was assistant in international law with the legal department of the International Monetary

Fund, in Washington DC and later attorney of the National Treasury of Brazil, at which time I participated in the government team which renegotiated Brazil's external indebtedness towards private sector creditors; finally, I joined a São Paulo-based law firm active in advising bank clients in contracting new indebtedness, this time under the form of bonds issued in international capital markets.

As a result of the research work undertaken in connection with the dissertation, it became clear to me that the contractual mechanisms that I was contemplating were by no means the sole, or even the principal, tool in debt management for private and public sector borrowers; market instruments such as derivatives became in time a more obvious technique of risk management. Yet, the initial impression which had motivated my research had resisted the test of critical analysis: adaptation mechanisms built into documentation evidencing financial transactions could well help avoid contractual disruptions such as those that had characterized the debt crisis of the 1980s. The following is the result of this academic endeavor.

INTRODUCTION

The ability of developing country borrowers to fulfill payment obligations under transnational financing transactions may be impaired by changes in circumstances beyond such borrowers' control. The developing country debt crisis of the 1980s underlined the link between external shocks and debt crises, in that it was prompted not only by erroneous policies adopted by debtor countries, but also by a combination of exogenous factors. Loan agreements concluded with commercial banks – the legal instrument which then predominantly evidenced developing country external indebtedness – provided no flexibility to cushion the adverse effects that external shocks had on borrowers' ability to fulfill contractual obligations.

This study submits that the legal framework for development financing transactions would be more sound if borrowers were allowed flexibility in performing payment obligations related to external indebtedness under adverse circumstances. The study suggests, through the analysis of specific contractual mechanisms, that adaptation of development financing transactions through the adoption of adjustment provisions can be both acceptable and desirable to borrowers and creditors alike. The former would gain on liability management, while the latter could derive financial benefits from provisions crafted to suit their particular needs. In addition, both sides would benefit from a contractual environment less vulnerable to shifts in factors beyond either party's control.

The survey undertaken in this study of specific adaptation provisions written into documentation relating to developing countries' debt restructuring agreements, further demonstrates

1

that there are legal techniques available which could evolve towards a more generalized adoption of adaptation clauses.

Adaptation of development financing transactions translates into adaptation of the instruments which evidence them. Loan agreements concluded between borrowers in developing countries and bank syndicates were the main instrument for development financing in the 1970s and early 1980s. Since then, debt in the form of bonds has replaced syndicated loan agreements as the main instrument documenting developing country debt, as a result of restructuring agreements entered in the course of the debt crisis, which entailed the exchange of bank credits for securities. In addition, bonds have also prevailed over bank loans in transnational lending since the resumption of private debt capital flows to developing countries. The issue of adaptation will be discussed in this study in connection with both loan agreements and bond issues.

In addition to contractually foreseen adaptation, adjustment of the terms of a financing transaction can be achieved through negotiation between a borrower and its creditors, as and when specific difficulties related to the fulfilment of parties' obligations arise. The debt crisis of the 1980s was characterized by such process of renegotiation of contractual obligations, leading to the conclusion of restructuring agreements, in a process of *ad hoc* contract adaptation which will also be reviewed in this study.

Developing country obligors under bank loans and bond issues in a transnational financing transaction range from private or public sector entities, government instrumentalities, to the sovereign itself. While measures related to the prevention of general liquidity crises ultimately pertain to the country's central government or central bank, individual public and private sector borrowers have a direct interest in managing their own liabilities as well. Unless otherwise indicated, the discussion of adaptation mechanisms undertaken in this study applies to all categories of borrowers within developing countries, and to the sovereign; the transactions involving all such categories of borrowers will be referred to in the aggregate as 'development financing'.

As regards creditors, the issue of adaptation will be discussed in connection with external financing transactions involving private sector banks, in the case of loan agreements, and investors at large, in connection with bond issues. Discussion of loan agreements concluded with official creditors or multilateral institutions will not be undertaken.

Part I of this study sets forth the general framework for the discussion of the issue of adaptation mechanisms in development financing. Part II addresses the core of this study, namely contractually foreseen adaptation, in the form of provisions written into documentation evidencing development financing transactions.

Part I:

ADAPTATION IN DEVELOPMENT FINANCING: GENERAL

Part I of this study sets forth the general framework for the discussion of adaptation in development financing. Chapter 1 describes the link between external shocks and debt crises, and surveys existing mechanisms, both market-based and institutional, for the protection of developing country debtors against adverse changes in circumstances, outside the realm of contract.

Chapter 2 discusses the terminology regarding adaptation, analyzes the types of contractual instruments to which the question of adaptation relates, namely loan agreements and documentation related to bond issues, and defines the scope of the study by stating the types of contractual relationships excluded from it.

Chapter 3 analyzes the process of *ad hoc* adaptation of borrowers' obligations in development financing that occurred in connection with the debt crisis of the 1980s.

Chapter One

DEVELOPMENT FINANCING AND EXTERNAL SHOCKS

This chapter is a general survey of the institutional and market-based mechanisms available to debt managers in developing countries seeking protection against the adverse financial impacts of external shocks. Before presenting the mechanisms available in the managing of external risks, the link between the occurrence of debt crises and changes in circumstances will be outlined.

Exogenous shocks and debt crises

A survey of the debt crises of the 1930s and of the 1980s reveals that, in addition to internal difficulties related to macroeconomic management, the problems were unequivocally prompted by exogenous factors as well.[1] Disagreement as to the relative role of internal and external factors notwithstanding, the fact is that both types of causes contributed to the causation of the crises.

In the latest developing country debt crisis, that of the 1980s, such conjuction of internal and external causes was clear. Poor resource allocation, investment decisions aiming at growth based on rapid accumulation of external debt, budget deficits and exchange rate policies leading to overvalued currencies and capital flight were among the internal factors which contributed to the problem.[2] In addition to such internal causes, exogenous

---

[1] The expression 'debt crisis' will be used throughout this study to designate generalized payment difficulties experienced by a given universe of borrowers.
[2] These factors are discussed in Cline, William R., INTERNATIONAL DEBT AND THE STABILITY OF THE WORLD ECONOMY, Washington DC, Institute for International Economics, 1983, 134p. (hereinafter Cline, INTERNATIONAL DEBT), at 26–29; and in the elaborate version by the same author, INTERNATIONAL DEBT: SYSTEMIC RISKS AND POLICY RESPONSES, Washington DC., Institute for International Economics, 1984, 336p. (hereinafter Cline, SYSTEMIC RISKS), at 14–17.

factors played a determinant role in causing the crisis.[3] Foremost were a surge in interest rates, currency exchange rate imbalances, and a deterioration in developing countries' terms of trade.

A mismatch between loose fiscal policy and tight monetary policy in the US drove up domestic – and international – interest rates.[4] Average real interest rates, obtained by deducting US inflation from nominal interest rates on outstanding long-term debt of developing countries, were a negative 6 percent for the period 1973–1977; the respective figure for the period 1981–1982 was a positive 3 percent.[5] Such rise in interest rates had a particularly perverse effect on borrowers' obligations due to the fact that outstanding debt had been contracted essentially at floating interest rates, as will be reviewed upon discussion of loan agreements.

In addition, the value of the dollar rose by 30–40 percent between the beginning of 1981 and the beginning of 1985;[6] since most of the outstanding debt was denominated in dollars, this rise represented a considerable additional burden to debtors.

While the two factors recalled above contributed to debtors' difficulties by magnifying the burden represented by debt payments, a third factor – a deterioration in the terms of trade

---

Cline points out that however serious the errors in domestic policies were:

it remains true that because the magnitudes of the external economic pressures on developing countries became so great (especially by 1981–1982), there was little margin left for domestic policy error. In evaluating domestic policy, it must also be kept in mind that the sharp decline in the global economy, rise in interest rates, and oil price shock of 1980–1982 were generally not predicted, and few would have advocated the extremely cautious borrowing policy that would have been consistent with foreknowledge of these global shocks.

Cline, SYSTEMIC RISKS, at 17.
[3]They were clearly identified in both of Cline's studies. See also Allsopp, Christopher, and Joshi, Vilai, *The Assessment – The International Debt Crisis*, i–xxxiii OXFORD REVIEW ECONOMIC POLICY vol. 2, n. 1, 1986 (hereinafter Allsopp, *The Assessment*); MANAGING FINANCIAL RISKS IN INDEBTED DEVELOPING COUNTRIES, IMF Occasional Paper no. 65, Washington DC, International Monetary Fund, June 1989, 47p. (hereinafter MANAGING FINANCIAL RISK), at 2–5; Lomax, David F., THE DEVELOPING COUNTRY DEBT CRISIS, New York, St Martin's Press, 1986, 317p., at 41–48.
[4]Cline, INTERNATIONAL DEBT, at 23; Cline, SYSTEMIC RISK, at 12.
[5]Cline, INTERNATIONAL DEBT, at 23; Cline, SYSTEMIC RISK, at 12.
    Nominal interest rates peaked 20% in 1982. Williamson, John, *The Outlook for Debt Relief or Repudiation in Latin America*, 1–6 OXFORD REVIEW OF ECONOMIC POLICY, vol. 2, n. 1 (1986) (hereinafter Williamson, *Relief or Repudiation*), 1–6, at 4.
[6]Allsopp, *The Assessment*, at xii.

– directly reduced borrowers' capacity to generate the foreign currency earnings with which to make such payments. The two oil crises of the 1970s led to a rise in the value of imports from 6 percent of total merchandise imports in 1973 to 20 percent in 1980–1982.[7] The severe recession which affected the world economy in 1980–1982, which was itself directly related to the rise in interest rates, had a further strong negative impact on developing countries' terms of trade and also on real export volumes.[8]

The combination of these adverse factors was described in the following manner:

> (...) it is well known that real interest rates were zero or negative for most of the 1970s, when Latin America was going into debt with the enthusiastic assistance of the commercial banks. They then rose to nominal rates that peaked at over 20 percent in the early 1980s. As nominal rates started to decline, so did inflation, so that real interest rates rose to as much as 8 percent if a US price index is used as the deflator and to very much more if prices of the debtor countries' traded goods are used. Moreover, the same shifts in the policies of the industrial countries that produced this historically unprecedented increase in the burden of interest service also produced a rise in the value of the dollar in which most debt is denominated, stagnation of export markets, falls in commodity prices, and protectionist pressures. In view of these facts one might have thought it reasonable for the industrial countries to have made some effort to ameliorate the costs borne by the debtors. Yet in fact they did the opposite and set about cutting back access limits and compensatory finance in the IMF without any offsetting expansion in the facilities of the World Bank.[9]

[7]Cline, INTERNATIONAL DEBT, at 20; Cline, SYSTEMIC RISK, at 8–9.
[8]Cline, INTERNATIONAL DEBT, at 24, and Cline, SYSTEMIC RISK, at at 12–13.
[9]Williamson, *Relief or Repudiation*, at 4. It is instructive to review concerns about the impact of external factors before the actual onset of the crisis. A study published in 1979 warned:

> If the debtor developing countries cannot expand their exports in order to repay their debts for reasons, it must be recalled, which are unrelated to the performance of their own economic policy makers, they must either find new sources of finance or undertake severe and politically disruptive domestic adjustments. The developing countries can be expected to resent creditors' demands for payment when they at the same time erect barriers to the

Exogenous factors had also clearly been at the origin of the generalized Latin American defaults of the 1930s. Then, the crisis had a direct relationship with the recession in the world economy and the decline in commodity prices and export revenues that it entailed. A classical study of sovereign defaults thus describes the causation link:

> Although financial mismanagement in various forms helped engender the wave of insolvencies which disrupted the contractual relations between borrowing states and their foreign creditors during the early 1930s, that cataclysm was largely attributed to circumstances beyond the debtors' control. The steep fall in prices and shrinkage of trade which characterized the world-wide economic slump was accompanied by an abrupt cessation of foreign loans. As a consequence debtor countries suffered a severe depletion of their foreign exchange resources and were obliged to suspend partially or wholly the service of their external debts in the creditors currencies.[10]

As the two passages cited above indicate, in the 1980s as in the 1930s the crisis was precipitated by an external factor of a subjective nature – namely, creditors' perception of the debt servicing difficulties encountered by debtors leading to a sharp retraction in lending.[11] The phenomenon was strikingly similar in the crises

---

means whereby debtors might earn the wherewithal with which to do so and offer no other assistance for economic malaise, political instability and substantially increased international unpleasantness.

Helleiner, G.K., *Relief and Reform in Third World Debt*, 113–124 WORLD DEVELOPMENT WORLD BANK, World Bank (1979) (hereinafter Helleiner, *Relief and Reform*), at 116.

[10]Borchard, Edwin, and Wynne, W.H., STATE INSOLVENCY AND FOREIGN BONDHOLDERS, vol. I, GENERAL PRINCIPLES, New York, Garland, 1983, 381p. (hereinafter Borchard, STATE INSOLVENCY), at 143.

Other studies pointed out the same causation link between the previous debt crises and external shocks. See Eichengreen, Barry, and Portes, Richard, *The Anatomy of Financial Crises*, 10–58 THREATS TO INTERNATIONAL FINANCIAL STABILITY (Richard Porter and Alexander K. Swoboda editors) Cambridge, Cambridge University Press, 1987, 307p. (hereinafter Eichengreen, *Anatomy of Crises*), at 20; Fishlow, Albert, *Lessons from the Past: Capital Markets during the 19th Century and the Interwar Period*, 383–439 INTERNATIONAL ORGANIZATION vol. 39, n. 3, (1985), at 428.

[11]The problem was aggravated by debtors' resorting to short-term debt, normally the only type of finance which remains available in a situation of imminent insolvency. Writing in 1982, one author noted the phenomenon:

of the 1930s and that of the 1980s. In the 1930s, 'defaults by a few countries caused investors to revise their expectations for continued debt service by others. International lending all but evaporated following Bolivia's January 1931 default (...)';[12] in the 1980s, in turn, 'borrowing rose to some critical point where banks took fright and refinance became difficult if not impossible'.[13]

Hence, the shocks that motivated the crises of the 1930s and the 1980s took the form of significant shifts in individual variables which bear direct relationship with borrowers' capacity to pay principal and interest on external debt: international interest rates, currency exchange rates, commodity prices. The use of instruments and techniques designed to cushion the impact of external shocks can arguably reduce the likelihood of situations of illiquidity which characterize debt crises. Such instruments and techniques will be surveyed in the following section.

Protecting against external shocks

A survey of the concerted course of action adopted by governments in debtor and creditor countries, international financial institutions and private sector creditors throughout the debt crisis of the 1980s, undertaken later in this study, reveals that debt management was then tantamount to debt restructuring.

Management of external liabilities was limited to the refinancing of debt and the rescheduling of maturities, both required as remedial measures, once it became evident that obligations could not be performed as provided for under the relevant agreements. Comprehensive debt management of a preventive nature

It is this buildup of short-term debt, well above the amounts normally associated with trade, that explains the apparent suddenness with which the problems of Argentina and Mexico have burst upon the international financial market. Both borrowers and lenders were in effect attempting to buy time, in the hope that interest rates would come down, and export earnings revive, in the wake of an often announced but, until now, not yet begun recovery of the business cycle in the United States and Western Europe. (...) At that point, sometime in mid-1982, a major retraction of lending took place.

Kuczynski, Pedro-Pablo, *Latin American Debt*, 344–364 FOREIGN AFFAIRS, winter 1982/1983, at 348.
[12]Eichengreen, *Anatomy of Crises*, at 22.
[13]Allsopp, *The Assessment*, at xiii.

was unfeasible in that context: the pressing imminence of default hindered, if it did not bar altogether, medium- and long-term planning.

It is fair to assume that a developing country whose external debt obligations have been restructured in a way that makes it possible for the country to define its external liabilities in the medium and long term is in a position to manage actively such liabilities in a preventive manner – as opposed to merely reacting to a situation of illiquidity. In a context of restructured external liabilities and foreseeable cash flows, debt management will ideally gain on the preventive side.

With the hindsight one now has of the debt crisis of the 1980s, there arises a fairly comprehensive picture of mechanisms that may enable indebted countries borrowing abroad to cope with financial risks related to exogenous factors. One category of such mechanisms is the main subject-matter of this study, namely the adaptation mechanisms that can be embedded in documentation related to developing country borrowing from private sources. The following sections will discuss the market-based instruments and the institutional mechanisms that make up the range of techniques available to debt managers in developing countries interested in ensuring protection against the adverse impact of external shocks.

Hedging instruments

Parties to a transnational transaction may obtain protection from the adverse effects of external shocks through the purchase of financial products available in the market-place, either in formal exchanges, or 'over the counter', in transactions entered with specialized institutions. Such products are commonly referred to as *hedging instruments*, by reference to the function they perform; or, more technically, as *derivative instruments*, which may be defined as 'financial contracts whose value depends on the values of one or more underlying assets or indexes'.[14] Such underlying assets or indexes may be, for instance, a commodity, or a currency or interest rate.

Hence, *forward contracts*, *futures*, *swaps* and *options* have been known to institutions in industrialized countries active in inter-

---

[14]Risk Management Guidelines for Derivatives, Basle Committee on Banking Supervision, July 1994, 19p., at 3 (hereinafter Risk Management Guidelines).

national transactions under which they are exposed to shifts in variables such as interest and currency rates and commodity prices, as a technique of asset and liability management.[15] Just as is the case with institutions in industrialized countries, the use of derivatives will in time, in all likelihood, become the main technique of risk management to borrowers from developing countries, a trend which is reinforced by the fact that the market for such financial instruments is in constant evolution.

The discussion of *contractually foreseen* adaptation, which is the essence of this study, stands in contrast to such possibility of attaining protection against external shocks through the use of market-based instruments. As will be seen in Part II of this study, the generalized adoption of adaptation mechanisms in development financing would amount to a departure from standard practice, and is not devoid of technical difficulties. In this sense, and from the viewpoint of economic analysis, the decision as to whether to seek protection through contract provisions or in the market-place entails an analysis of cost efficiency. Hence, if it is less costly to buy an interest rate cap and thus hedge against sharp rises in interest rates than to insert an interest capping provision in the relevant agreement, the former course should be the decision of the debt manager in charge.

This study concedes that the resort to market-based instruments should indeed be the *main* risk management technique adopted in the future by debt managers in developing countries under voluntary financing transactions. Other things being equal, it also seems reasonable to assume that the resort to derivatives is likely to be more cost-efficient than the devising of contractual mechanisms to the same effect; this economic analysis falls beyond the scope of this study.

The discussion of contractually foreseen adaptation finds its

---

[15]On the financial instruments used, see generally *Recent Instruments in International Banking*, Bank for International Settlements (BIS), April 1986, 270p., at 37–126; De Covny, Sheree, and Tacchi, Christine, HEDGING STRATEGIES, New York, Woodhead Faulkner, 1991, 202p.

The techniques of asset and liability management were initially used by financial institutions in industrialized countries to control unexpected downturns in income related to interest, later being used by other types of institutions to hedge against risks related to exchange rates and commodity prices as well. Masuoka, Toshiya, ASSET AND LIABILITY MANAGEMENT IN THE DEVELOPING COUNTRIES. MODERN FINANCIAL TECHNIQUES, World Bank Working Paper WPS 454, Washington DC, World Bank, 1990, 56p. (hereinafter Masuoka, ASSET AND LIABILITY MANAGEMENT), 4.

justification, however, whenever unhindered resort to market-based instruments does not exist. This seems to be the case with respect to development financing.[16] A number of constraints are commonly cited as limiting the actual availability of such mechanisms to parties in developing countries. The high costs involved in the operations which imply disbursements up-front, such as options contracts; the lack of an institutional framework, comprising specialized labor, to manage complex hedging operations; constraints related to maximum maturities traded and market liquidity, given the fact that the market for derivatives is still relatively recent; and, last but not least, doubts regarding the creditworthiness of the parties in developing countries which severely limit their access to markets for such instruments in the first place.[17]

Few developing country borrowers which could potentially use such risk-hedging derivatives were actually in a position to do so throughout the 1980s, which were characterized by a succession of debt restructuring packages and little room for medium-term planning in debt management. A country which had accumulated interest arrears and was about to work out a restructuring package – the resulting debt profile of which was yet unknown – did not have predictability as to its cash flows, a prerequisite for liability management. The list of developing country debtors that have actually undertaken asset and liability management corroborates this fact.[18]

[16]Even in those instances where access – if limited – to derivatives is ensured, it can be resorted to *in conjunction with* the inclusion of adaptation provisions in agreements governing external indebtedness, as a means to optimize liability management. Furthermore, the widespread use of derivatives itself involves risks, as evidenced by great losses experienced by actors involved in large-scale transactions, as well as by efforts on the part of government authorities, both at national and supranational levels, to adopt a regulatory and supervisory framework for derivatives markets; see RISK MANAGEMENT GUIDELINES. These issues fall beyond the scope of this study, and will not be discussed here.

[17]See MANAGING FINANCIAL RISKS IN INDEBTED DEVELOPING COUNTRIES. IMF Occasional Paper No. 65, Washington DC, International Monetary Fund, June 1989, 47p. (hereinafter MANAGING FINANCIAL RISKS), at 17; Lessard, Donald R., and Williamson, John, FINANCIAL INTERMEDIATION BEYOND THE DEBT CRISIS, Washington DC, Institute of International Economics, September 1985, 118p. (hereinafter Lessard, FINANCIAL INTERMEDIATION), at 73–74; Masuoka, ASSET AND LIABILITY MANAGEMENT, at 43–49.

[18]The list reveals either countries which did not restructure their private sector debt – India, Indonesia, Turkey – or countries such as Chile and Mexico, which had attained apparently lasting solutions to their external debt difficulties at the time the transactions were entered.

The latest round of developing country debt restructuring, described later in this study, could help set the stage for increased strategic, long-term debt planning on the part of developing country debtors, should it provide a lasting solution to the external debt problem. The fact that most of the hindering factors mentioned above are of a conjunctural nature and can therefore be overcome with time, as well as the maturing of the market for derivatives, should contribute to the diversification of developing countries' management of external liabilities.

In time, the market for derivatives can present an effective alternative for liability management at the level of individual corporate borrowers within developing countries, as well as to public sector entities.[19] However, the use of hedging instruments by a large sovereign debtor in its overall debt management strategy will probably remain an unrealistic proposition, given the magnitude of the amounts involved as well as the difficulties in finding counterparties to match the underlying credit risk. Significant portions of restructured developing country debt remain in floating rate form.[20] At least as far as hedging against interest rate risk is concerned, market-based transactions are likely to continue playing a marginal role only. This would seem to underline the importance of building interest rate protection mechanisms, such as the ones discussed in this study, into the agreements themselves.

In the following, different types of risk-hedging mechanisms will be briefly described.

Forward contracts   A forward contract is an agreement to pur-

---

For a picture of LDC utilization of risk-hedging market instruments in 1988 and 1989, see Table 12 (*External Risk Management in Developing Countries*) of IMF Occasional Paper no. 77, DETERMINANTS AND SYSTEMIC CONSEQUENCES OF INTERNATIONAL CAPITAL FLOWS, Washington DC, IMF, March 1991, 94p., at 42; and Masuoka, ASSET AND LIABILITY MANAGEMENT, at 31–40.

[19]The latter can expect to receive technical support in this regard from the World Bank, which is itself very active in using such techniques in the management of its own liabilities. Indeed, the Bank seems to have started 'exporting' its own expertise to interested member countries. Masuoka, ASSET AND LIABILITY MANAGEMENT, at 50–51. See also Wallich, Christine I., *The World Bank's Currency Swaps*, FINANCE & DEVELOPMENT, June 1984.

[20]This is true even after the Brady restructuring agreements which turned a large portion of developing country external indebtedness into fixed rate form due to a marked preference on the part of creditors for the fixed rate par bond option, as described below.

chase or sell a given asset at a future date at a pre-set price; the asset can be a commodity, a given currency or a rate of interest.

A forward contract allows its buyer to eliminate uncertainty with regard to future revenues or costs by 'locking-in' the price of an asset. If the ultimate spot, or market price for the asset in question is higher than the pre-determined price upon maturity of the forward contract, the seller of the asset fails to make a profit; he will nevertheless have achieved predictability as to his cash flow. Hence, an exporter who is also a borrower under a dollar-denominated agreement and whose main source of revenues are denominated in German marks may wish to lock-in the rate of the dollar against the mark by entering into a forward contract.[21]

Forward contracts are carried out 'over the counter', through brokers and dealers, rather than in formal exchanges. To the extent that forward contracts do not require cash transfers up-front other than transaction fees, they involve a credit risk, an aspect which limits the access of this instrument to developing country borrowers.[22] Also, markets for forward contracts are only liquid up to a certain maturity, which in practice limits the use of this instrument for long-term liability management.[23]

Futures contracts   As with forward contracts, parties entering a futures contract agree to purchase/sell a given asset at a given date at a given price. Unlike forward contracts, which are traded over the counter, futures are standardized agreements which are traded in formal exchanges. Also, profits and losses are settled daily – so as to prevent a party from carrying a significant loss over a long period of time – thereby reducing credit risk. This daily settlement of profits and losses is made possible by a so-called 'margin' deposit which parties to futures contracts are required to make with the exchange.

As with forward contracts, futures contracts exist for major currencies, interest rates and commodities.[24]

---

[21]For a discussion on the use of forward contracts by LDC debtors, see Masuoka, ASSET AND LIABILITY MANAGEMENT, at 14–16.

[22]Masuoka, ASSET AND LIABILITY MANAGEMENT, at 43.

[23]Masuoka, ASSET AND LIABILITY MANAGEMENT, at 16.

[24]For discussion on the use of futures by LDC borrowers, see Masuoka, ASSET AND LIABILITY MANAGEMENT, at 16–18.

Swaps Swap contracts are agreements under which parties commit to exchange a series of specified payment obligations denominated in one currency for a series of specified payment obligations denominated in a different currency (currency swaps); or to exchange a series of specified payment obligations determined by reference to a fixed rate of interest for a series of specified payment obligations determined by reference to a floating rate of interest, or vice versa (interest rate swaps).

Thus, a borrower with dollar-denominated debt and revenues mostly in German marks may enter a currency swap agreement with a bank in order to exchange its German-mark revenues for dollar amounts at a pre-specified exchange rate, thus controlling the effects of exchange fluctuations that might otherwise impair its ability to meet its dollar-denominated payments under its debt obligations. Likewise, a borrower with floating rate debt may enter an interest rate swap with a bank whereby it commits to pay a fixed rate of interest calculated over a notional amount; the bank will, in exchange, pay the borrower interest at a floating rate, which interest the borrower will then use to service its own original loan.[25]

Swap contracts, which are arranged through traders and brokers or traded in formal exchanges, do not require cash exchanges up-front; in this sense, they involve a credit risk, a factor which impacts its availability to developing country borrowers. Swaps markets are liquid for relatively long maturities, thereby making these instruments effective tools for strategic debt planning.

Interest rate swaps Under an interest rate swap agreement, parties commit to respond reciprocally for payment of the interest due by the other party on the basis of a theoretical loan, the amount of which is determined by mutual accord.[26] A developing debtor country with floating interest rate obligations thus hedges against adverse fluctuations in the reference rate of interest. The following description of an interest rate swap helps illustrate the potential benefit of this instrument:

In an interest rate swap, the indebted developing country

[25]For a discussion on the use of swaps by borrowers in developing countries, see Masuoka, ASSET AND LIABILITY MANAGEMENT, at 21–23.
[26]EXCHANGE RATE RISKS IN INTERNATIONAL CONTRACTS, Paris, ICC Institute, 1987, 431p. (hereinafter EXCHANGE RATE RISKS), at 12.

would make a stream of fixed rate interest payments and receive a stream of floating rate payments over an agreed time period, while the counterpart (usually a bank) would receive fixed, and make floating payments. No actual principal would be exchanged either at the beginning or at the termination of the contract. A floating rate borrower can thus achieve any desired medium-term lengthening of this interest rate period using an interest rate swap. Although the market is an over-the-counter market, a significant amount of standardization in swap contracts has added greatly to liquidity in this market.[27]

Currency swaps Currency swaps, in turn, help hedge against unfavorable fluctuations in exchange rates. To the extent that a given country's external obligations are predominantly denominated in one major foreign currency, currency swaps can be an efficient risk-hedging instrument.[28] Under a currency swap agreement, the parties undertake to exchange sums of two different currencies over a certain period at a pre-specified rate. The mutual advantage of such a transaction usually derives from the comparative advantage the two parties have on the market for each currency in question: a borrower whose revenues are mainly denominated in dollars arguably has an advantage in having its liabilities also denominated in that same currency.[29] The potential advantages are clear:

[27]MANAGING FINANCIAL RISKS, at 10. See also Kalderen, Lars, *Techniques of External Debt Management*, 99–111 EXTERNAL DEBT MANAGEMENT (Hassanali Mehran editor), Washington DC, IMF, 1985, 322p., especially at 107–110.

[28]Developing countries' ability to make efficient use of currency swaps can be impaired by *currency switching*, or *currency conversion* provisions included in restructuring packages entered with commercial bank creditors. Under such provisions, creditor banks are given the right to change the currency denomination of the loans at regular intervals. By bringing in an element of uncertainty to the currency composition of the borrower's external indebtedness, currency switching provisions can thus reduce their ability to hedge against currency risks. On currency switching mechanisms, see Lamdany, Ruben, *The Market-Based Menu Approach in Action: The 1988 Brazilian Financing Package*, 163–175 DEALING WITH THE DEBT CRISIS (Ishrat Husain and Ishac Diwan editors), World Bank, 1989, 308p., at 164.

[29]As pointed out in a study by the International Chamber of Commerce, '[parties] decide to enter into this kind of operation because one of them has better access to one market (e.g. that of the dollar) whilst the other has better access to another (e.g. that of the Swiss franc)', EXCHANGE RATE RISKS IN INTERNATIONAL CONTRACTS, Paris, ICC Institute, 1987, 431p., at 16. On currency and interest rate swaps, see also ASSET AND LIABILITY MANAGEMENT BY BANKS, Paris, OECD, 1987, 176p., at 69–70.

(. . .) a significant contributory cause to the debt crisis was the reduction in the dollar value of developing country exports induced by the dollar appreciation, which eroded the ability to service debts that were predominantly dollar-denominated. One way of avoiding this risk would have been to contract debts in a bundle of currencies that matched the destination of exports. A simpler technique now potentially available is to swap dollar debt-service liabilities for liabilities in a bundle of currencies that matches the currencies of price determination of the country's net exports.[30]

Options The buyer of an option contract acquires the right to buy or sell a certain asset at a pre-set price on or before a specified date. An option to sell a certain asset is a 'put' option; an option to buy an asset is a 'call' option.[31] Whether such buyer will or will not exercise such right will depend primarily on whether the pre-set price is superior – in the case of a call option – or inferior – in the case of put options – to the spot price at the time of expiration of the option.

Unlike forward and future contracts, there is no 'locking-in' of the price of the asset in question; instead, against payment of a premium up-front, the buyer of an option acquires the opportunity to take advantage of favorable price movements for the underlying asset, or, conversely, to hedge against unfavorable price movements.[32]

Call options on interest rates are called caps, whereas put options on interest rates are called floors: by giving its purchaser the right to buy or sell the interest rate once the market rate hits a pre-determined maximum or minimum level, option contracts

---

[30]FINANCIAL INTERMEDIATION, at 73.

Currency swap transactions for developing countries are expressly encouraged by the World Bank in connection with its Enhanced Cofinancing Operations program. The Bank claims one of the advantages of ECO is currency flexibility:

This enables borrowers to target the financing to obtain the chosen currency; arrange swaps of the borrowed currency(ies) of choice; and better manage the liability composition of the borrower's indebtedness.

The World Bank Expanded Cofinancing Operations, Washington DC, World Bank Cofinancing and Financial Advisory Services, January 1991, 4p., at 1–2.

[31]Masuoka, ASSET AND LIABILITY MANAGEMENT, at 18–19.

[32]For a discussion on the use of options by developing countries, see Masuoka, ASSET AND LIABILITY MANAGEMENT, at 18–21.

effectively enable a borrower to minimize the effects of variations in the market interest rates upon its own obligations.

Option contracts are offered both formally, in exchanges, as well as informally, through traders and brokers. A premium must be paid up-front for the option. Option contracts exist not only for interest rate and currencies, but also for commodities.

Institutional mechanisms

The International Monetary Fund's Contingency and Compensatory Financing Facility, as well as the STABEX scheme of the Lomé Conventions are institutional arrangements designed to provide financial assistance to developing countries that have suffered external shocks which affect their balance of payments position.[33]

Unlike market-based instruments, discussed above, compensatory and contingency mechanisms under the norms of the International Monetary Fund and the Lomé Conventions are not tools for the regular management of liabilities available to private and public sector borrowers on a commercial basis. Instead, they amount to institutional mechanisms set up in multilateral arenas, to be used under exceptional circumstances to cope with financial imbalances at the official level, by central governments. A brief discussion of their main features is relevant to this study, however, to the extent both mechanisms were conceived to address problems related to developing country exposure to external shocks.

The IMF's Compensatory and Contingency Financing Facility (CCFF)
The law is familiar with concepts of *force majeure* or unforeseeable supervening circumstances or events. A somewhat similar idea runs through certain policies of the IMF under which members receive positive benefits rather than release

---

[33]See *Compensatory Financing of Export Earnings Shortfalls*, Report of the Expert Group of the UNCTAD, New York, United Nations, 1985, TD/B/1029/Rev. 1 (hereinafter *Compensatory Financing*). The report reviews other institutional efforts made in the same direction, such as international commodity agreements and World Bank lending designed to offset export shortfalls. In 1965 the Bank put forward a scheme to provide financial resources in a somewhat institutionalized manner to developing countries in times of export earnings shortfalls. Implementation of this scheme was abandoned for lack of support from prospective donors; *Compensatory Financing*, at 19.

from obligations. The idea is that circumstances or events beyond a member's control can have detrimental effects on its balance of payments, and then the IMF should provide resources that help to mitigate the harm and prevent the possible danger.[34]

As a result of calls for a comprehensive treatment of external contingencies on the part of the IMF,[35] agreement was reached in the 1988 spring meeting of the Interim Committee of the Fund to establish a comprehensive facility that would comprise the matters of compensatory and contingency financing.[36] In that meeting it was recognized that:

> as the time horizon of programs supported by the Fund has lengthened with the growing complexity of problems facing Fund members, exogenous shocks of an unpredictable character could endanger successful implementation of a program supported by the Fund.[37]

[34]Gold, Joseph, *Natural Disasters and Other Emergencies Beyond Control: Assistance by the IMF*, 621–641 THE INTERNATIONAL LAWYER, fall 1990 (hereinafter Gold, *Natural Disasters*), at 621.

[35]See Griffith-Jones, Stephany, *Ways Forward from the Debt Crisis*, 39–61 OXFORD REVIEW ECONOMIC POLICY vol. 2, n. 1 (1986) (hereinafter Griffith-Jones, *Ways Forward*), at 43–45; Bergstein, C. Fred, Cline, William R. and Williamson, John, BANK LENDING TO DEVELOPING COUNTRIES: THE POLICY ALTERNATIVES, Washington DC, Institute for International Economics, 1985, 210p. (hereinafter Bergstein, BANK LENDING), at 75–76.

[36]On the IMF in general, see the course given at the Hague Academy of International Law by the General Counsel, Gianviti, François, *The International Monetary Fund and External Debt*, 209–286 RCADI 1989 III (hereinafter Gianviti, *The International Monetary Fund*); and former General Counsel Gold, Joseph, FINANCIAL ASSISTANCE BY THE INTERNATIONAL MONETARY FUND: LAW AND PRACTICE, IMF Pamphlet Series, no. 27. Washington DC, IMF, 2nd edition 1980. For an overview of Fund operations, see Petersmann, Hans G., FINANCIAL ASSISTANCE TO DEVELOPING COUNTRIES: THE CHANGING ROLE OF THE WORLD BANK AND THE INTERNATIONAL MONETARY FUND. INSTITUTIONAL, LEGAL AND POLICY PERSPECTIVES, Bonn, Forschungsinstitut der Deutschen Gesellschaft für Auswärtige Politik e.V., 1988, 123p. (hereinafter Petersmann, FINANCIAL ASSISTANCE), at 24–55; and FINANCIAL ORGANIZATION AND OPERATIONS OF THE IMF, by the Treasurer's Department of the International Monetary Fund, IMF Pamphlet Series, no. 45. Washington DC, IMF, 119p., 1990.

The Interim Committee is a consultative organ to the Board of Governors of the IMF which meets usually twice a year to discuss the major current issues; Gianviti, *The International Monetary Fund*, at 218.

[37]*Fund Establishes Compensatory and Contingency Financing Facility*, Press Release no. 88/25, August 26, 1988, 275 IMF SURVEY, vol. 17, no. 17, August 29, 1988 (hereinafter *Fund Establishes Facility*).

In August 1988 the CCFF was established.[38] This new facility replaced previously existing compensatory financing facilities, and created a novel contingency financing window.

The existing facilities replaced by the CCFF were the Compensatory Financing Facility (CFF) for Export Fluctuations, established in 1963,[39] and the Facility for Financing of Fluctuations in the Cost of Cereal Imports, created in 1981.[40] Both had been designed to help IMF members deal with balance of payments difficulties considered to be of a temporary and reversible character and which therefore required emergency financing rather than adjustment.[41] Such assistance would thus discourage members from resorting to exchange and trade restrictions.[42]

The main features of the CCF were preserved under the compensatory portion of the novel CCFF. Under the latter, as under the previous CCF, a member's request for assistance will be attended 'if the shortfall in export earnings is of a short-term character and is largely attributable to circumstances beyond the control of the member';[43] in addition, the country is requested to adopt appropriate measures designed to fight the balance of payments difficulties.

The novel element in the CCFF is its contingency portion. At the time a member country concludes a stand-by or extended arrangement with the Fund,[44] it may request that a contingency

[38]Decision No. 8955–(88/126), of August 23, 1988. SELECTED DECISIONS AND SELECTED DOCUMENTS OF THE INTERNATIONAL MONETARY FUND, 16th issue, May 31, 1991, at 136–163.

On the CCFF in general, see Pownall, Roger, and Stuart, Brian, *The IMF's Compensatory and Contingency Financing Facility,* 9 FINANCE AND DEVELOPMENT, December 1988 (hereinafter Pownall, *CCFF*).

[39]On the CCF, see Goreux, Louis M., CONTINGENCY FINANCING FACILITY, IMF Pamphlet Series no. 34, 1980, 84p.

[40]In addition to the export and to the cereals facilities, the Fund established in 1969 a buffer stock financing facility to help finance members' contributions to buffer stock schemes. *Compensatory and Contingency Financing Facility Helps Members Adjust to External Shocks,* 12 IMF Survey 19, August 1990 (hereinafter *Compensatory and Contingency*).

[41]*Fund Establishes Facility,* at 275.

[42]Gold, *Natural Disasters,* at 628.

[43]§11 (a) of the Decision.

[44]Gold defines a stand-by arrangement as:

'a decision of the Fund that gives a member the assurance that it will be able to make purchases of the Fund's general resources (. . .) during a specified period and up to a specified amount. (. . .) The terms of the decision (. . .) make the member's ability to go on making purchases in the higher credit tranches dependent on the member's observance of certain policies or practices that are elements in the program.'

mechanism be included under the CCFF. The contingency financing mechanism may also, under special circumstances, be attached to arrangements under the structural adjustment facility (SAF) as well as under the enhanced structural adjustment facility (ESAF).[45]

The contingency mechanism provides for financing to cover part of the net adverse effect on the member's balance of payments caused by unfavorable deviations in key current account variables such as export revenues, import prices and international interest rates, that are volatile and easily identifiable.[46] A central element of the mechanism is that such deviations must be beyond the member's control.

The arrangement providing for contingency financing will typically outline, among other elements, the exogenous factors to be covered, the price and other projections on the basis of which deviations will be estimated, and the threshold that the deviations must cross so that the mechanism can be triggered, as well as the proportions of given contingencies that can be financed. Hence, the contingency mechanism will be triggered once net deviations in the elements defined as the exogenous factors exceed the specified threshold level and it becomes clear that movements in current account variables not covered by the mechanism have not offset the deviations.

In the language of the Fund's decision which established the facility:

> Such external contingency financing will only be provided in association with a Fund arrangement, generally on the basis of a review by the Executive Board, to a member facing

Gold, Joseph, *Relations Between Bank's Loan Agreements and Fund Stand-by Arrangements*, 781–802 Gold, Joseph, LEGAL AND INSTITUTIONAL ASPECTS OF THE INTERNATIONAL MONETARY SYSTEM (1984) (hereinafter Gold, *Relations between Bank and Fund*) at 88. Extended arrangements are usually subject to the Fund's policy governing stand-by arrangements. However, they differ from stand-by arrangements in two regards at least: they are longer – usually three years, as opposed to one year under a stand-by arrangement; and they are designed to provide assistance associated with structural maladjustments. Gold, LEGAL ASPECTS, at 787 and 789.

[45]§10 of the Decision. Under the SAF and ESAF facilities, the Fund provides low-income countries with relatively long-term assistance on terms which are more concessional than those of the ordinary reserve tranche transactions. SAF funds come from sales of gold subscriptions, while ESAF resources are originated from loans and donations of members. Gianviti, *The International Monetary Fund*, at 256; Petersmann, FINANCIAL ASSISTANCE, at 52–55 and 72–73.

[46]*Compensatory and Contingency*, at 12.

unanticipated deviations from the baseline projections of key external variables that cover a substantial proportion of the exogenous components of the member's current account and that relate to the specified external contingencies during the period of the projections (hereinafter called the 'baseline period'), if:

the deviations from the baseline projections are outside of the control of the member;

the member's performance under the associated Fund arrangement is satisfactory; and

the member is prepared to adapt its adjustment policies as may be necessary to ensure the viability of the program supported by the associated arrangement through a mix of adjustment and financing appropriate to the circumstances of the member.[47]

The external contingency financing will generally not exceed 70 percent of the amount of the associated Fund arrangement.[48] In the case of changes in interest rates, contingent financing is subject to a supplementary limit of 35 percent of the member's quota.[49] Disbursements under the CCFF, which come from the Fund's ordinary resources, will take place at the time of the disbursements under the associated – stand-by or extended – arrangement, and will have a repayment period of three to five years.[50]

The rationale of the contingency financing portion of the CCFF is to help a member country in difficulties over balance of payments caused by the advent of adverse external circumstances. Conversely, the contingency mechanism envisages the scenario in which these external factors change in a way that is favorable

[47]§ 18 of the Decision creating the CCFF.
[48]§ 22 of the Decision.
[49]§ 21 of the Decision. According to Pownall and Stuart, this stricter limit to which Fund financing of deviations in international interest rates under the CCFF is subject, is explained by a desire to 'avoid possible adverse implications for the Fund's liquidity from changes in interest costs', as well as to encourage member countries 'to hedge or cover the interest rate risk of part of their foreign debt or otherwise reduce the variability of interest costs through existing market mechanisms'. Pownall, *CCFF*, at 10.

According to Gold, this provision was apparently adopted in response to the argument that increases in interest rates are not wholly beyond a member's control, to the extent that the member country has voluntarily undertaken to pay variable interest rate under the debt contracted; Gold, *Natural Disasters*, at 632.
[50]§ 25 (b) of the decision. Pownall, *CCFF*, at 10 and 12.

to the member's balance of payments position. In this event, the member would be expected, under a 'symmetry' provision included in the arrangement, to set a portion of the gain from the favorable deviation to its international reserves so as to strengthen its external position. Alternatively, it may be provided that the member begin repaying earlier contingency financing disbursements. A third variation of the 'symmetry' provision has the Fund reducing disbursements under the associated stand-by or extended arrangement.[51] This 'symmetry' provision in arrangements with the Fund under the CCFF bears resemblance to and follows the same 'benefit-sharing' rationale of provisions on reduction of commitments and prepayment of advances included in agreement with commercial banks, discussed later in this study.[52]

The STABEX mechanism under the Lomé Conventions The IMF's Contingency and Compensatory Financing Facilities have a global character, in that all developing countries member to the Fund are, as a matter of eligibility, entitled to draw on the facilities. At a more limited geographical level, in turn, the STABEX scheme under the Lomé Convention linking the European Economic Community to Africa, the Caribbean and Pacific (ACP) countries also seeks to provide stabilization of developing countries' export earnings, i.e. protection against sharp fluctuations in hard currency revenues. Four Lomé Conventions have been signed to date. Lomé IV, signed in December 1989, covers the period 1990–2000 and links the EEC and 68 ACP states.[53]

The STABEX scheme was established with the first Lomé Convention, in 1975, and has been revised under the subsequent

[51]On the 'symmetry' provision, see Pownall, *CCFF*, at 11 and *Fund Establishes*.
[52]Criticism of the CCFF centered on the required degree of conditionality, which is more stringent than under the CCF. Gold draws attention to the fact that the language used in the Fund decision creating the CCFF denotes that the facility 'was adopted with some trepidation' (Gold, *Natural Disasters*, at 631). He further notes that 'the section of the CCFF on external contingencies, however, is formulated with such complexity and detail, and at such length, that members, unable to understand all the intricacies of this policy, have been deterred from resorting to it' (Gold, *Natural Disasters*, at 639).
[53]1990 *Development Cooperation Report*, Paris, OECD; at 144. Lomé IV was signed on December 15, 1989. The text of Lomé IV Convention is reproduced in 29 ILM 783 (1990).

agreements.[54] STABEX seeks to stabilize export earnings by providing transfers in convertible currencies to ACP countries having suffered earnings shortfalls, related either to price or to volume, on exports to the European Community of products on which their economies are particularly dependent. Article 186 of Lomé IV provides:

> With the aim of remedying the harmful effects of the instability of export earnings and to help the ACP States overcome one of the main obstacles to the stability, profitability and sustained growth of their economies, to support their development efforts and to enable them in this way to ensure economic and social progress for their peoples by helping to safeguard their purchasing power, a system shall be operated to guarantee the stabilization of export earnings derived from the ACP States' exports to the Community or other destinations as defined in Article 189, of products on which their economies are dependent and which are affected by fluctuations in price or quantity or both these factors.

The mechanism is therefore geographically limited – to exports from ACP countries, to the European Community; and it is linked to export earnings shortfalls of one particular commodity, rather than to a decrease in overall export revenues.[55]

STABEX transfers shall be devoted 'either to the sector, in the

---

[54]STABEX was accepted by EEC States, among other reasons, as an alternative to mechanisms 'involving buffer stocks, market intervention, and common funding between commodities'. To that extent, STABEX 'provided the EEC with a substantial initiative on commodity stabilization while not committing the Community to "common funding" approaches and financial disbursements to put this into effect', Hewitt, Adrian P., *Stabex and Commodity Export Compensation Schemes: Prospects for Globalization*, 617–631 WORLD DEVELOPMENT, vol. 15, no. 5, 1987 (hereinafter Hewitt, *Stabex*), at 619. Meanwhile, UNCTAD was developing the 'Common Fund' approach for the stabilization of commodity prices, which however did not become effective. See on the Common Fund *Compensatory Financing*, p. 20–22.

[55]This partial coverage of the STABEX mechanism – only ACP countries are eligible; only agricultural commodities can trigger the transfers; and only exports to the EEC are contemplated – is the source for the most serious criticism of the scheme. Hewitt, *Stabex*, at 625.

A separate mechanism under the Lomé Conventions, the *Sysmin* scheme, addresses the problem of shortfalls related to the export of minerals. Article 214 of Lomé IV provides:

> A special financing facility shall be set up for those ACP States whose mining sectors occupy an important place in their economies and are facing difficulties that are already perceived or foreseeable in the near future.

widest possible sense, that recorded the loss of export earnings', or, 'where appropriate, to diversification'.[56] Under previous Lomé Conventions, ACP States which received transfers were, under certain conditions, expected to contribute to the replenishment of the fund in subsequent years;[57] an exception to this repayment obligation was provided for in favor of the least-developed countries. However, under Lomé IV STABEX transfers have been converted into grants under the Lomé IV Convention.[58]

---

[56]Article 186, 2. of Lomé IV.
[57]*Compensatory Financing*, at 20.
[58]Article 240, 1.(b) of the Convention provides that 'STABEX transfers will be granted without any obligation for the beneficiary ACP States to reconstitute the resources of the system.'

Chapter Two

THE CONCEPTUAL FRAMEWORK

This chapter sets forth the conceptual framework for the discussion of adaptation in development financing. First, the question of terminology related to the issue of adaptation is discussed. The contractual instruments in respect to which adaptation applies are then reviewed. Finally, those types of development financing transactions excluded from the scope of this study will be surveyed.

Adaptation: terminology

'Adaptation' is a broad term which may take different meanings according to the context in which it is applied. The discussion undertaken in this chapter is limited to those meanings which are relevant for the two contexts where it is applied here – namely, contractually foreseen adaptation; and *ad hoc* adaptation in the context of the debt crisis.

As applied to provisions of an agreement, 'adaptation' is a comprehensive term designating a wide range of clauses which provide contractual flexibility by adjusting the terms of the agreement to circumstances which alter the initial contractual balance.

The topic of adaptation and renegotiation clauses in international agreements is the object of abundant literature.[59]

[59]Boughaba, Mohammed, LES CLAUSES D'ADAPTATION ÉCONOMIQUE ET MONÉAIRE DANS LES CONTRATS PRIVÉS INTERNATIONAUX, Lausanne, Entlebuch, 1984, 356p. (hereinafter Boughaba, CLAUSES D'ADAPTATION), in particular 253–323; van Dunné, Jan M., *Adaptation by Renegotiation – Contractual and Judicial Revision of Contracts in Cases of Hardship*, 413–439 THE COMPLEX LONG-TERM CONTRACT. STRUCTURES AND INTERNATIONAL ARBITRATION (Fritz Nicklisch, editor), Heidelberg, C.F. Müller, 1987, 597p. (hereinafter van Dunné, *Adaptation by Renegotiation*); Fouchard, Philippe, *Adaptation of Contracts to the Economic Climate*, 6–73/6–89

Although efforts have been made to establish a typology of adaptation clauses,[60] the wide range of contractual fields from which the sample clauses used in the studies undertaken to date have been drawn makes this a difficult task; the same obstacle makes more difficult the search for standard terminology.

A variety of possible classifications exists, and there is logic to most. Thus, adaptation provisions can be classified based on whether they relate to procedure or to substantive results.[61] In

---

ARBITRATION AND THE LICENSING PROCESS (Robert Goldscheider and Michel de Haas, editors). New York, Clark Boardman Co. Ltd., 1984 (hereinafter Fouchard, *Adaptation to the Economic Climate*); Gold, Joseph, LEGAL EFFECTS OF FLUCTUATING EXCHANGE RATES, Washington DC, IMF, 1990, 473p. (hereinafter Gold, FLUCTUATING EXCHANGE RATES), at 226–247; Horn, Norbert, *Standard Clauses on Contract Adaptation in International Commerce*, 111–140 ADAPTATION AND RENEGOTIATION OF CONTRACTS IN INTERNATIONAL TRADE AND FINANCE (Norbert Horn editor), Antwerp, Kluwer, 1985, 421p. (hereinafter Horn, *Standard Clauses on Contract Adaptation*); van Ommeslaghe, Pierre, *Les Clauses de force majeure et d'imprévision (hardship) dans les contrats internationaux*, 7–59 REVUE DE DROIT INTERNATIONAL ET DE DROIT COMPARÉ (1980); Oppetit, Bruno, *L'adaptation des contrats internationaux aux changements de circonstances: la clause de 'hardship'*, 794–814 JOURNAL DU DROIT INTERNATIONAL (1974) (hereinafter Oppetit, *L'Adaptation des contrats internationaux*); Peter, Wolfgang, ARBITRATION AND RENEGOTIATION OF INTERNATIONAL INVESTMENT AGREEMENTS. A STUDY WITH PARTICULAR REFERENCE TO MEANS OF CONFLICT AVOIDANCE UNDER NATURAL RESOURCES INVESTMENT AGREEMENTS, Dordrecht, Martinus Nijhoff, 1986, 297p. (hereinafter Peter, ARBITRATION AND RENEGOTIATION), in particular 148–166; and, by the same author, *Adaptation and Renegotiation Clauses*, 29–46 JOURNAL OF INTERNATIONAL ARBITRATION vol. 3, n. 2 (1986) (hereinafter Peter, *Adaptation and Renegotiation*); Schmithoff, Clive M., *Hardship and Intervener Clauses*, 415–423 CLIVE M. SCHMITHOFF'S SELECT ESSAYS ON INTERNATIONAL TRADE LAW (Chia-Jui Cheng editor), 1988 (hereinafter Schmithoff, *Hardship Clauses*); Ullman, Harold, *Enforcement of Hardship Clauses in the French and American Legal Systems*, 81–106 CALIFORNIA WESTERN INTERNATIONAL LAW JOURNAL, vol. 19 (1988) (hereinafter Ullman, *Enforcement of Hardship Clauses*).

[60]Horn, *Standard Clauses on Contract Adaptation*, at 121–122.

[61]Peter comments on such a classification:

A strict and consistent classification might distinguish between terms that describe a procedure and terms that describe a result. Such classification would, however, be unusual and create a risk of misunderstanding or additional difficulties.

Peter, ARBITRATION AND RENEGOTIATION, at 148; see also Peter, *Adaptation and Renegotiation*, at 30.

The present author does not see how such classification would necessarily create additional difficulties; on the contrary, it is a logical one which has the advantage of providing the flexibility required in the discussion of adaptation clauses, given the wide range of fields to which they apply.

Such distinction is also implicitly acknowledged by Horn:

In the following list of standard clauses we will be content to distinguish

this sense, renegotiation clauses can be differentiated from adaptation clauses *stricto sensu* – a first general division which will be adopted in this study.

Adaptation clauses can alternatively be fitted under different categories based on the extent of the contractual modifications they propose,[62] or classified according to the magnitude of the changes which trigger them.[63] It is equally conceivable to classify provisions based on the character of the triggering event – whether general or specific.[64]

Although the different analyses of adaptation provisions at large have great relevance and analytical use for the study of adaptation provisions related to development lending, any general theoretical framework cannot be justified, it is submitted, on the basis of intrinsic characteristics. This is because the range

---

three main groups of clauses which either lead to an automatic adaptation or trigger a renegotiation.

Horn, *Standard Clauses on Contract Adaptation*, at 122.

[62]Hence, Peter proposes the distinction between *adaptation* clauses – 'provisions that allow contract changes by following an automatic or pre-determined pattern or which are merely designed for the filling of gaps in the contract'; *force majeure* clauses, 'clauses which produce radical change as they terminate or suspend the further carrying out of the contract'; and *renegotiation* clauses, 'clauses which require a common effort of the parties to agree, for various reasons, to a substantial material change of the contract to an extent usually determined at the time of conclusion'. Peter, ARBITRATION AND RENEGOTIATION, at 148.

[63]According to Horn,

[the distinction] can be made according to the nature and weight of the events contemplated and their impact of the contract. The first group comprises clauses relating to 'minor' or 'natural' events which the parties cannot completely foresee but take into account as a normal element in long-term transactions. The clauses of this group constitute what we can describe as a 'built-in contractual flexibility'. Other events of considerable weight and impact on contractual liabilities lead to more fundamental changes in the contract. Here, we have to distinguish between events which reduce or terminate contractual liability and those which define a breach of contractual obligations.

Horn, *Standard Clauses on Contract Adaptation*, at 122. The list that follows such comments in his article, however, does not seem to fit the description. Instead, it gives the reader the impression of an enumeration of clauses which at times present little relation to an adaptation provision; one such example is that of default and cross-default provision, which the author includes in his discussion.

[64]Boughaba, CLAUSES D'ADAPTATION, at 270–271; Fouchard, *Adaptation to the Economic Climate*, at 6–76:

The adaptation clauses might aim at special circumstances or, on the contrary, be drafted in a general form. General adaptation clauses provide for the possibility of a modification of the contract without stipulating strictly or in details the new circumstances motivating this.

and nature of adaptation clauses in a particular field of law reflects the specific needs and characteristics of the transaction which they relate to, and are tailored to the instruments that embody them. The peculiarities of each field of international agreements helps explain why most typologies actually resemble enumerations of concrete clauses.

The classification which provides the structure for the discussion undertaken in Part II of this study attempts to meet the peculiarities of the field of financing transactions involving developing country debtors. A general distinction will be made between clauses related to procedure and to substance; hence, the discussion of *renegotiation* clauses will precede that of *adaptation* clauses *stricto sensu*. The latter are to be understood in the present context as clauses providing for automatic contract adaptation.

Adaptation clauses *stricto sensu* will in turn be discussed according to the party whose obligations are subject to adaptation, as well as to the nature of the changes they contemplate. Provisions which propose adapting the obligations of borrowers will be discussed separately from those regarding adaptation of lenders' obligations.

Within each broad category of clauses, provisions will be presented according to the nature of the changes proposed. Hence, in the case of adaptation of borrowers' obligations, interest capping and interest capitalization provisions will be discussed jointly under a heading regarding provisions addressing interest rate risk; and separately from clauses linking *obligation* to pay to *capacity* to pay. In the case of adaptation of lenders' obligations, contingency financing will be distinguished from provisions entailing reduction in commitments.

As in a general discussion on adaptation clauses, the application of adaptation to the field of international development lending transactions entails a discussion of triggering events; the consequences of adaptation, and third party intervention. These topics will be examined upon discussion of each specific category of provisions.

With respect to *ad hoc* adaptation in connection with the debt crisis, the literature on the topic of debt restructuring does not present uniformity as to the terms used regarding the phenomenon of adaptation of borrower's obligations. The following working definitions seem to conform to the terminology generally used, and will be applied in this study.[65]

The term debt 'restructuring' will be used in a generic sense, being interchangeable with 'adaptation' or 'modification'; hence, the expression 'restructuring agreements' will be used in reference to agreements concluded by debtor countries with the universe of their commercial bank creditors to adjust the terms of the original loan agreements, including maturities, interest rates and fees. 'Rescheduling', in turn, is to be understood as the change in the terms of a loan agreement which specifically entails a modification of the original maturities of the debt, including the adoption of new grace periods. Finally, 'refinancing' will be used to designate the extension of new funds under a restructuring agreement, regardless of the form – credit agreement or bond issue – that the financing takes.

The subject-matter of adaptation: loans and bonds

Adaptation of borrowers' obligations takes place in the environment provided by the documentation pursuant to which those obligations arise. In the 1970s and early 1980s, until the advent of the debt crisis, medium- and long-term loan agreements concluded with syndicates of commercial banks constituted the main instrument for the channeling of financing from private sources to developing country borrowers. With the onset of the debt crisis, bank lending to developing countries came to a complete halt except for loan commitments in connection with debt restructuring exercises.

As a result of such restructuring agreements entered in connection with the debt crisis, described later in this study, bonds have replaced loan agreements as the main instrument evidencing developing country debt, as a consequence of the exchange of

[65]See Hudes, Karen, *Coordination of Paris and London Club Reschedulings,* 553–571 NEW YORK UNIVERSITY JOURNAL OF INTERNATIONAL LAW AND POLITICS vol. 17 (1985), footnote 23, at 560:

Bank debt restructuring is defined here to cover both the rescheduling and refinancing of debt service payments in arrears (generally principal repayments). (. . .) Rescheduling is a formal deferral of debt service payments over a period exceeding one year, with new maturities applying to the deferred amounts. Refinancing is either a straight rollover of maturing debt obligations or involves the conversion of existing and/or future debt service payments into new medium-term loans.

outstanding claims for new instruments, in the form of bonds. This primacy of bond debt over bank loans is reinforced by the fact that bond issues have prevailed over bank loans in the context of resumed access of developing country borrowers to international capital markets.

The following is a discussion of the features of bank loans and bond issues which are relevant for the ensuing survey of *ad hoc* adaptation through restructuring agreements, as well as the discussion of specific types of adaptation provisions.

Loan agreements

Medium- to long-term loan agreements concluded with private sector banks were the legal instrument at the base of the large-scale process of developing country transnational borrowing from commercial sources which characterized development financing in the 1970s and early 1980s.[66] The following consists of a discussion of the main features of such instruments and of the hindrances to their use in development financing in the future.

Features Under such loan agreements, banks were usually organized under a syndicate, for reasons related to the volumes of financing involved. Bank syndicates were formed because the loan amounts were often larger than one single bank could

---

[66]On the topic of international loan agreements, see in general Wood, Philip, LAW AND PRACTICE OF INTERNATIONAL FINANCE, London, Sweet & Maxwell 1980, 462p. (hereinafter Wood, INTERNATIONAL FINANCE), at 233–256; Venkatachari, K., *The Eurocurrency Loan: Role and Content of the Contract*, 73–122 SOVEREIGN BORROWERS. GUIDELINES ON LEGAL NEGOTIATIONS WITH COMMERCIAL LENDERS (Lars Kalderen and Qamar S. Siddiqi editors), London, Butterworths, 1984, 264p. (hereinafter Venkatachari, *Eurocurrency Loan*); Logan, Francis D., and Rowntree, Peter D., *Term Loan Agreements*, 1–14 I INTERNATIONAL FINANCIAL LAW. LENDING, CAPITAL TRANSFER AND INSTITUTIONS (Robert S. Rendell editor), London, Euromoney, 1983, 200p. (Logan, *Term Loan Agreements*); Nurick, Lester, *Negotiation of Transnational Bank Loan Agreements Entered into by Developing Country Borrowers: Legal and other Issues*, 43–79 ISSUES IN NEGOTIATING INTERNATIONAL LOAN AGREEMENTS WITH TRANSNATIONAL BANKS, New York, United Nations Centre on Transnational Corporations, 1983, ST/CTC/48, 103p. (hereinafter Nurick, *Negotiation of Loan Agreements*); Adede, A.O., *Legal Trends in International Lending and Investment in the Developing Countries*, 9–168 RCADI 1983–II (hereinafter Adede, *Legal Trends*), at 27–75.

handle, for economic or legal reasons related to lending limits.[67] Such loans extended to developing country borrowers were generally unsecured. They were called 'general purpose', or 'balance of payments' loans because, from a formal standpoint, they were not extended in order to finance any specific project or transaction, and borrowers were free to use the loan proceeds as they found fit. Funds were made available to the borrower for an agreed period of time, with disbursement of the loan amounts usually completed in the early life of the loan.[68]

Along with the financial terms of the loan agreements such as loan amount, interest rate, maturity and amortization schedule, the legal provisions in a syndicated loan agreement invariably included representations and warranties, conditions precedent to drawdown, covenants and events of default – including a provision regarding cross default, i.e. default under other external indebtedness triggering a default under the loan agreement into which the clause was written.

In seeking comfort against the fact that they were entering an agreement with a foreign borrower, creditors derived legal comfort from the inclusion of a choice of law clause, usually for New York or English law,[69] as well as a choice of forum clause usually conferring jurisdiction upon courts sitting in the state of New York or London, depending on the applicable law. In case the borrower was the sovereign itself, or some instrumentality thereof, such as the Central Bank, choice of law and jurisdiction

---

[67]Semkow, Brian W., *Syndicating and Rescheduling International Financial Transactions: A Survey of the Legal Issues Encountered by Commercial Banks*, 869–927 International Lawyer, vol. 18, n. 4, fall 1984 (hereinafter Semkow, *Syndicating*), at 869.

[68]However, flexibility regarding disbursement could be obtained, if required, through the conclusion of revolving credits, under which the borrower could borrow, repay, and then reborrow again during the life of the loan, up to an agreed amount. Alternatively, a stand-by loan was possible, entitling the borrower to drawdown funds at any time up to a specified limit. See Semkow, *Syndicating*, at 891–892.

[69]See Logan, Francis D., *Term Loan Agreements*, 11–23 INTERNATIONAL FINANCIAL LAW. LENDING, CAPITAL TRANSFERS AND INSTITUTIONS (Robert S. Rendell editor), London, Euromoney, 1980, 304p., at 17.

One author analyzing a representative sample of agreements states that 'of the agreements analyzed, about one half were governed by New York law, almost one half by United Kingdom law, and the balance by French, Federal Republic of Germany, Japanese, Luxembourg, Ontario and Swiss law, and in two cases by local law (Colombia and Venezuela)', Nurick, *Negotiation of Loan Agreements*, at 71.

clauses would be complemented by provisions regarding waiver of immunities.[70]

Syndicated loan agreements typically provided for contractual flexibility in the form of a set of provisions which protected lenders from changes in circumstances; parallel protection was unavailable to borrowers. Such unilateral flexibility was justified by the fact that lenders under a financing transaction were vulnerable once disbursement was made, and as such required protection from subsequent changes in circumstances.

The first such mechanism, indeed a salient feature of loan agreements concluded with private sector banks, was the provision for floating interest rate, which would typically be the London Interbank Offered Rate (LIBOR), or the prime rate.[71] The fact that the interest rate was floating, not fixed, was related to the method by which banks funded the loan. Banks borrowed in the interbank market at short term – usually three to six months – and on-lent the funds to the final, developing country borrower under a medium- or long-term agreement. Since the interest rate in this interbank market would be set at the end of every term, which was shorter than that of the related transaction with the developing country borrower, the floating interest rate clause built into the loan agreement with the developing country

[70]The degree to which foreign sovereigns submitted to the jurisdiction of foreign courts, as well as the scope of waiver of immunity clauses would vary, however. See Nurick, *Negotiation of Loan Agreements*, at 72. The Federative Republic of Brazil, for instance, does not submit to the jurisdiction of foreign courts, and settlement of dispute clauses included in agreements to which it is a party provide for arbitration. This is in Brazil a matter of law as much as of practice, since passage of Senate Resolution 82 of December 1990, which required the provision for arbitration as the means for dispute settlement in international agreements to which the Republic or its instrumentalities are a party.

[71]Wood, INTERNATIONAL FINANCE, at 253:

The essence of the eurocurrency floating rate loans is the manner in which the loans are funded by the lender. In order to make a loan a bank borrows matching funds from other banks in the market for on-lending. These funding deposits are taken for short terms such as 3, 6 or 12 months (interest periods) and at the end of each interest period the bank pays back the underlying deposit and immediately reborrows another deposit for a further period. The interest rate payable by the ultimate borrower will be a specified percentage, known as the 'spread' or 'margin' (which represents the gross profit and remuneration for the risk), above the rate at which the bank borrows the underlying deposits from other banks in the London interbank market.

debtor constituted an effective and essential protection for lenders.[72]

The term loan agreement with the developing country borrower would specify interest periods, equivalent to the prevailing funding structure of the relevant creditors; the rate valid for the period would be determined a few business days prior to the commencement of the relevant interest period, and would consist of the reference rate then prevailing. Lenders' remuneration consisted of a spread, or margin, added to the reference interest rate.[73]

Additional provisions sought to protect the position of lenders against a series of conceivable events. Hence, *yield protection* clauses provided that the borrower indemnify the lender against the costs resulting from the imposition of any reserve or special deposit requirements, as well from any change in the basis for taxation of the lender.[74] *Illegality clauses*, in turn, provided for immediate prepayment of the loan in case the performance of lenders' obligations became unlawful by virtue of supervening legislation, or government action. Alternatively, it could be stipulated that the parties try to reach a substituted basis of disbursement.[75] Finally, *market disaster* clauses provided for the same consequences – renegotiation aiming at a substituted basis

---

[72]According to the study by Harvey,

> [without] variable interest rates on loans, the capacity of eurocurrency banks to convert mainly short-term deposits into medium-term loans would have been much less, the growth of this form of lending to developing countries would also have been much smaller, and the deficit countries would almost certainly have had to cut back even further on imports than they actually did – with appalling effects on production, employment, income and welfare.

Harvey, Charles, *On Reducing the Risk in Foreign Finance – For Both Parties*, Institute for Development Studies Discussion Paper no. 167, November 1981, 160p. at 3; this is a pioneer study which will be referred to several times in the following, as Harvey, *Reducing the Risk*.

[73]See Crozer, George K., and Wall, Duane D., *The Eurodollar Market: Loans and Bonds*, 63–78 INTERNATIONAL FINANCIAL LAW. LENDING, CAPITAL TRANSFER AND INSTITUTIONS (Robert Rendell editor). London, Euromoney, 1980, 319p. (hereinafter Crozer, *The Eurodollar Market*), at 63–64.

[74]Crozer, *The Eurodollar Market*, at 64; Wood, INTERNATIONAL FINANCE, at 255.

The content of yield protection clauses will also encompass the requirement that all payments be made net of any withholding taxes or other charges; and that the borrower reimburse the lender for losses – related to interest rate differentials – incurred as a result of prepayment. Crozer, *The Eurodollar Market*, at 64.

[75]Crozer, *The Eurodollar Market*, at 64.

of borrowing, or termination with prepayment – for the event that the lender's ability to fund the loan be impaired or hindered by some disruption of the market.[76]

It would be interesting to verify to what extent and in how many instances clauses protecting lenders from changes in circumstances were of effective use. Whatever the case, they are a clear illustration that concerns with changes in the circumstances which were present at the time of conclusion of the agreement led drafters to build in to the contracts some mechanisms which provided for relief, even though such concerns were unilateral, and resulted in contractual protection in favor of lenders only.

Indeed, unlike creditors, borrowers under syndicated bank credits were unprotected against subsequent changes in circumstances. Such scarce in-built flexibility prevailed despite the medium- to long-term duration of the agreements and the wide range of external contingencies to which parties are subject to during the life of the loan.

The lack of flexibility of loan agreements was underlined in connection with the debt crisis, when borrowers' contractual obligations remained unchanged despite the occurrence of a set of external shocks, reviewed above, which directly impaired their ability to fulfill payment obligations. This rigidity of syndicated loan agreements contrasts with the flexibility which can be found under instruments used in other fields of international transactions, as will be recalled in Part IV (Chap. 6) of this study.[77]

The apparent rigidity of transnational development financing bank credits presents a parallel with domestic loan agreements entered by financial institutions with corporate borrowers, in that the latter do not contain provisions protecting borrowers from changes in circumstances either. Given the nature of the

[76]Nurick, *Negotiation of Loan Agreements*, at 51–52; Wood, INTERNATIONAL FINANCE, at 254; Crozer, *The Eurodollar Market*, at 64.
[77]The existence of adaptation clauses in favor of lenders might give the misleading impression that term loan agreements were a model of contractual flexibility:

> Syndicated loans are a fine example of built-in contractual flexibility. Their interest rates are floating according to a commonly used formula. (. . .) Such a formula is the most common instrument used to shift to the borrower the interest risk flowing from the transformation of short-term loans into medium-term loans. Other contractual provisions serve the same purpose.

Horn, Norbert, *Standard Clauses on Contract Adaptation in International Commerce*, 111–140 ADAPTATION AND RENEGOTIATION OF CONTRACTS IN INTERNATIONAL TRADE AND FINANCE (Norbert Horn editor), Antwerp, Kluwer, 1985, 421p.) (hereinafter Horn, *Standard Clauses on Contract Adaptation*), at 119.

respective obligations of parties under a loan transaction, this was probably perceived to be in the normal course of things. Once disbursements are made, the creditor has little bargaining power *vis à vis* the borrower, and accordingly requires protection from subsequent changes in the contractual environment.

However, the floating interest rate structure, with which commercial banks were also familiar because of domestic financing transactions under which they were a common feature, proved to be flawed under transnational financing transactions involving developing country borrowers. It transferred entirely on to debtors the risk of interest rate fluctuation. Should sharp increases in the interbank rates occur, the burden would be borne by the end borrower[78] – which is precisely what occurred in the debt crisis, as discussed in the introduction to this study.[79]

While such fluctuations in interest rate could, in theory at least, be cushioned nowadays through the use of market-based derivatives, these were unavailable and unknown to developing country borrowers at the time of the debt crisis, and the impact of dramatic changes in interest rates was accordingly magnified. The adverse effects of such fluctuations could also be mitigated through the use of escape valves in the form of adaptation provisions dealing with interest rate fluctuations; this is precisely the main scope of this study, and the question will be discussed in Part II below.

Constraints to continued bank lending through loan agreements
While syndicated loan agreements were the main instrument for the channeling of financing for developing country borrowers

---

[78]Such transfer of the burden to borrowers is underlined in the following passage:

> [The widespread use of roll-over credit] was an attempt to separate interest risk from liquidity risk and to allow banks to engage in maturity transformation without incurring interest-rate risk. But in the process it shifted interest-risk to borrowers, made their debt-service costs unpredictable and thus potentially worsened credit risk.

ASSET AND LIABILITY MANAGEMENT BY BANKS, OECD, Paris, 1987, 176p., at 47.
[79]Lessard, FINANCIAL INTERMEDIATION, at 3, states:

> The invention of the rollover loan with a floating interest rate seemed at the time to be a marvelous development from the standpoint of lenders, but it turned out that the resulting concentration of risk on the borrowers was more than they could absorb. When the world economy imposed a series of adverse shocks on them in the early 1980s, the borrowers had no option but to seek extensive rescheduling.

in the 1970s and early 1980s, the prospects for their playing such a prominent role in development financing in the near future are meager. Reasons related to creditworthiness, profitability and bank regulation indicate that private sector banks active in transnational business will refrain from offering services related to the financing of developing country borrowers.

Interestingly enough, a survey conducted shortly before the onset of the latest developing country debt crisis among 52 leading international banks pointed out that the main constraints foreseen to the growth of international lending in the years ahead were credit risk, capital adequacy requirements and the profitability of international as against domestic lending.[80] A World Bank study published around the same time arrived, in the main, at the same conclusion: future bank lending to developing countries would essentially depend on the evolution of a few specific factors – namely, profitability, country lending limits, country risk perceptions, capital adequacy, and the regulatory framework.[81] All of these factors have since developed in a markedly adverse manner that is likely to lead to a sharp reduction in commercial bank involvement in credit transactions with developing country borrowers.

Country risk

The disruptive experience of the debt crisis unequivocally buried creditors' perception that a sovereign would never go bankrupt,[82] which played an important role in the lending boom of the 1970s. Accordingly, from the onset of the debt crisis onwards, commercial bank lending to developing countries was limited to refinancing provided in connection with restructuring agreements.

[80]*The Outlook for International Bank Lending*, M.S. Mendelsohn, editor, Washington DC, Group of Thirty, 1981, 51p. (hereinafter *The Outlook*), at 4.
[81]O'Brien, Richard R., PRIVATE BANK LENDING TO DEVELOPING COUNTRIES: PAST, PRESENT AND FUTURE, World Bank Staff Working Paper no. 482. Washington DC, World Bank, August 1981, 54p. (hereinafter O'Brien PRIVATE BANK LENDING, at 28–29.
[82]The statement is attributed to Walter Wriston, former chief executive officer of Citicorp; according to an account of the debt crisis, the expression used by Wriston was actually that countries 'don't go out of business' ('Banking Against Disaster', NEW YORK TIMES, September 14, 1982); Lissakers, Karin, BANKS, BORROWERS AND THE ESTABLISHMENT. A REVISIONIST ACCOUNT OF THE INTERNATIONAL DEBT CRISIS, New York, Basic Books, 1991, 308p., at 182.

Banks' frustration was prompted by persistent difficulties on the part of debtors to fulfill payment obligations, resulting in the need for continued restructuring exercises necessary to alleviate imminent interest payment difficulties, to reschedule principal installments and also, in some cases, to clear interest arrears.[83]

After a decade of strenuous talks around a negotiating table to restructure outstanding claims, commercial bankers' enthusiasm for extending fresh credits to borrowers in developing countries is simply non-existent. From a prospective viewpoint, the fact that much of the external indebtedness of restructuring developing countries has been transformed into collateralized securities in connection with Brady-type restructuring agreements, discussed below, makes bank lending unattractive *vis à vis* bond debt, given the perception related to the seniority of bonds, also discussed below.[84]

Profitability

Profitability of bank lending to developing country borrowers has likewise eroded since the onset of the debt crisis. Through the restructuring process, spreads and fees were gradually reduced after it became clear that restructuring exercises tended to repeat themselves, and that higher spreads and fees contributed in an important manner to increase the external financing gap that the debtor country had to cover.[85]

As regards United States commercial banks, which were

[83]See also DETERMINANTS AND SYSTEMIC CONSEQUENCES OF INTERNATIONAL CAPITAL FLOWS, IMF Occasional Paper no. 77. Washington DC, IMF, March 1991, 94p. (hereinafter DETERMINANTS OF CAPITAL FLOWS), at 38.

[84]'[There is a perception] that unsecured bank debt would be treated as a relatively junior claim if countries encountered renewed debt-servicing difficulties in the future', PRIVATE MARKET FINANCING FOR DEVELOPING COUNTRIES, World Economic and Financial Surveys. Washington DC, International Monetary Fund, December 1992, 80p. (hereinafter PRIVATE MARKET FINANCING), at 5.

[85]INTERNATIONAL CAPITAL MARKETS, DEVELOPMENTS AND PROSPECTS, IMF World Economic and Financial Surveys, Washington DC, IMF, April 1990 (hereinafter INTERNATIONAL CAPITAL MARKETS), at 29. Stumpf, Mark H., and Debevoise, Whitney, *Overview of Techniques: Raising New Money, Growth Facilities, Cofinancing and Collateralized Borrowings*, 53–75 LATIN AMERICAN SOVEREIGN DEBT MANAGEMENT. LEGAL AND REGULATORY ASPECTS (Ralph Reisner, Emilio J. Cardenas and Antonio Mendes editors), Washington DC, Inter-American Development Bank, 1990, 273p. (hereinafter Stumpf, *Overview of Techniques*), at 58; see also Cline, William R., MOBILIZING BANK LENDING to DEVELOPING COUNTRIES, Washington DC, Institute for International Economics, 1987, 92p. (hereinafter Cline, MOBILIZING BANK LENDING), at 51–53.

among the main players involved, profitability was further affected as a consequence of the passage of legislation after the advent of the crisis which hindered the profitable practice of front-end loading various fees charged in connection with the extension of a credit or the entering of a restructuring agreement.[86]

The regulatory framework

While perceptions as to country risk and profitability can be somewhat volatile factors, with developing countries regaining creditworthiness and profitability being restored under changed market circumstances, bank regulations amount to constraints of a more permanent nature that each bank must carefully consider before making any credit decision.[87] In this regard, a more permanent deterrent to renewed commercial bank lending to developing countries relates to the adoption by industrialized countries, in 1988, of the Basle Accord on capital adequacy, as a result of which it has become more costly for banks to keep in their books loans extended to developing country borrowers, relative to borrowers within the OECD.[88]

The *Proposals for International Convergence of Capital Measurement and Capital Standards*, also known as the Basle Guidelines or Basle Accord, were prepared by the Basle Committee on Banking Regulations and Supervisory Practices operating within the Bank for International Settlements and gathering representatives of

[86]International Lending Supervision Act of 1983, Pub. L. No. 98–181, 97 Stat. 1153, 1278 (codified at 12 USCA §§ 3901–3912 (1983)).

For a thorough discussion of the issue of profitability of US commercial banks in connection with LDC lending and the debt crisis, see Lichtenstein, Cynthia C., *The US Response to the International Debt Crisis: the International Lending Supervision Act of 1983*, 401–434 VIRGINIA JOURNAL OF INTERNATIONAL LAW (1985), in particular at 426–432.

[87]A detailed analysis of the process of debt creation in the 1970s and debt management in the 1980s would clearly demonstrate how commercial bank behavior is, in the field of cross-border lending as well, directly conditioned by the regulatory and accounting environment. See Hay, Jonathan, and Paul, Nirmaljit, REGULATION AND TAXATION OF COMMERCIAL BANKS DURING THE INTERNATIONAL DEBT CRISIS, World Bank Technical Paper Number 158, World Bank, Washington DC, 1991, 216p. (hereinafter Hay, REGULATION OF BANKS); TRANSNATIONAL BANKS AND THE EXTERNAL INDEBTEDNESS OF DEVELOPING COUNTRIES. IMPACT OF REGULATORY CHANGES, United Nations Document ST/CTC/SES.A/22. New York, United Nations, 1992, 48p.

[88]Although some developing countries have been admitted to the OECD, as is the case of Mexico.

central banks and supervisory authorities from twelve industrialized countries.[89] The proposed rules, setting minimum capital adequacy standards for banks undertaking significant cross-border business, are ultimately aimed at strengthening the international financial system, as well as at leveling out competitive inequality among international banks which derive from differences in individual countries' supervisory requirements.[90]

The method adopted in the guidelines for assessing capital adequacy consists in defining 'capital'; allocating specific assets to certain risk-categories, so as to arrive at 'risk-weighted' assets; and establishing a target standard ratio of capital to weighted risk assets. The latter, to be achieved at the end of the transitional period of five years, was set at 8 percent, of which the 'core capital' element should be at least 4 percent. 'Tier one' capital, or 'core capital', comprises equity capital and disclosed reserves. 'Tier two', or supplementary capital, includes undisclosed reserves, revaluation reserves, general loan loss reserves, hybrid debt capital instruments and subordinated term debt.

The process by which assets are allocated different degrees of risk under the guidelines involves an assessment of credit risk, or the risk of counterparty failure to fulfill its obligations under

---

[89]The first version of the Basle Agreement is reproduced at 27 ILM 524 (1988). The document will be referred to as *Proposals*.

The Basle Committee is composed of representatives of central banks and supervisory authorities of the 'Group of Ten' countries, actually composed of eleven countries (Belgium, Canada, France, Germany, Italy, Japan, Netherlands, Sweden, Switzerland, United Kingdom and the United States) and Luxemburg. This body is frequently referred to as the 'Cooke Committee', after the name of its initial chairman.

For a general discussion of the capital adequacy rules, see Norton, Joseph Jude, *The Multidimensions of the Convergence Processes Regarding Prudencial Supervision of the International Banking Acts – The Impact of the Basle Supervisors' Committee Efforts Upon, Within and Without the EC*, 249–324 FESTSCHRIFT JOSEPH GOLD, Heidelberg, Recht und Wirtschaft, 1990, 470p.

On the specific issue of the impact of the new rules on LDC lending, see Roberts, Steven M., *Capital Adequacy and LDC Debt: The Impact of the Basle Agreement*. TRENDS AND FORCES IN INTERNATIONAL BANKING LAW Seminar, Bern 26–30 March 1990, 15p., processed; Smith, Carsten, and Follak, K.P., *The New Capital Standards of International Banks: Support or Obstacle to Development Aid and External Debt Management*, Paper included in the report of the Committee on International Monetary Law of the International Law Association at the 1990 Conference Conference (Australia), 14p.

[90]See the *Introductory Note* by Cynthia Lichtenstein, 27 ILM 524 (1988), 524–527.

The document provides that 'each country will decide the way in which the supervisory authorities will introduce and apply these recommendations in the light of their different legal structures and existing supervisory arrangements', *Proposals*, §51.

any given credit agreement.[91] Claims which are perceived as conveying little risk, either because the debtor in question is perceived as highly creditworthy, or because of the nature of the asset, are assigned a low weight. Thus, claims against the domestic central government, for instance, are assigned a zero weight. By contrast, assets which involve a higher credit risk attract higher weights; hence, commercial credits in general are assigned a weight of 100 percent.

The practical impact of the process of assigning a high-risk weight to particular assets was clear: such assets 'require' comparatively larger capital than an asset carrying a zero or a low-risk weight – or, in other words, they have to be matched by a larger amount of capital. Assets carrying low-risk weights are favored over those attracting a high-risk weight, in that they allow enhanced use of the capital base to be used/applied as leverage the institution's activities.

Under the Basle risk weights, claims against central governments, public sector entities and banks outside the OECD countries are assigned the highest, 100 percent risk factor. The original version of the Basle Guidelines, issued in December 1987, did not convey a definitive proposal implying a distinction between claims against OECD and non-OECD countries. The *Proposals* put forward two possible solutions – namely, a simple differentiation between claims on the domestic public sector and all cross-border claims on the public sector; or, alternatively, 'an approach involving the selection of specific countries with high credit standing in some defined grouping and the application of low weights to cross-border claims on the public sector (and banks) of those countries'.[92]

The revised document, issued in July 1988, reported that 'the comments submitted to the Committee by banks and banking

---

[91]The guidelines provide for their own amendment so as to include an assessment of – and accordingly require capital adequacy in relation with – interest rate risk as well. § 32 of the document.
The original focus on credit risk is explained in the following terms:

> Traditionally, banks have invested most of their funds in illiquid assets such as secured and unsecured loans to costumers funded by highly liquid deposits and borrowings and by capital. Banks traditionally have held these assets to maturity, and therefore, the credit risk is the most important risk that bank regulators must address.

SYSTEMIC RISKS IN SECURITIES MARKETS, Paris, OECD 1991, 64p., at 45.
[92]§ 31(b) of the *Proposals*.

associations in G-10 countries during the consultative period were overwhelmingly in favour of the second alternative'. Decisive was the consideration that

> a simple domestic/foreign split effectively ignores the reality that transfer risk varies greatly between different countries and that this risk is of sufficient significance to make it necessary to ensure that broad distinctions in the credit standing of industrialized and non-industrialized countries should be made and captured in the system of measurement, particularly one designed for international banks.[93]

Hence, the Basle Guidelines are likely to have a lasting inhibiting effect on LDC lending, even though developments in financial markets can help the structuring of transactions which minimize such constraints.[94]

Bond issues

With the marked retraction of, and meager prospects for, bank lending to developing countries, the issuance of bonds again became the main form of developing country transnational borrowing with the resumption of capital flows to developing countries.[95]

The expression 'bond' designates any type of negotiable security. In practice, 'bond issues' may translate into a wide

[93]§ 34 of the revised *Proposals*.
[94]For instance through the pledge of securities issued by OECD countries as collateral for non-OECD securities. Also, developments in the securities industry allow financial institutions to repackage claims in the form of bank credits and sell them in the form of securities, thereby avoiding the negative regulatory implications of holding the assets in the books. This could be done, for instance, by transferring the credits to a special purpose vehicle, the capital of which would be paid for with the credits against the LDC borrower. Such institution could subsequently issue securities representing indebtedness of its own. Interview with commercial bank official, New York, January 25, 1993.
[95]Such a replacing of bank loan debt by bond debt in development financing parallels the similar evolution in worldwide capital markets. See RECENT INSTRUMENTS IN INTERNATIONAL BANKING, Basle, Bank for International Settlements (BIS), April 1986, 270p., in particular at 130–140.
On the regained access of developing country borrowers to international securities markets, see PRIVATE MARKET FINANCING; Fedder, Marcus J.J., and Mukherjee, Mohua, *The Reemergence of Developing Countries in the International Bond Markets*, 63–119 BEYOND SYNDICATED LOANS. SOURCES OF CREDIT FOR DEVELOPING COUNTRIES (John D. Shilling, editor), World Bank Technical Paper Number 163. Washington DC, World Bank, 1992, 119p.

variety of debt instruments, such as fixed or floating rate notes, hybrid instruments also comprising an equity feature, and others.

The predominance of bond debt over bank credits as the main instrument evidencing developing country external indebtedness was reinforced by the process of securitization that characterized the latest phase of debt restructuring agreements concluded in the course of the debt crisis, as reviewed below. Under this process, claims included in the restructuring exercise – usually in the form of bank credits – were exchanged for bonds issued by the restructuring country government.

The documentation involved in a bond issue is more complex than under a bank loan.[96] Loan agreements were typically crafted in an environment which featured a high degree of deregulation, as well as sophisticated financial institutions in the role of creditors. Under bond issues, in contrast, securities regulations intervene in order to impose disclosure, and possibly registration, requirements designed at protecting the investors, who may ultimately be the public at large, i.e. unsophisticated 'creditors'.[97] The fact that investments in securities are usually *managed* on behalf of ultimate bondholders by sophisticated professional portfolio managers does not eliminate the need for such requirements, since securities law cannot assume that every and each investor in bonds will benefit from professional investment advice.

The very nature of a bond transaction requires a wider set of agreements to govern the activities and relationship between the several players involved.[98] An offering circular, or a prospectus, is prepared in order to fulfill disclosure requirements,[99] containing information which is material in the context of the offering and issue of the instruments, comprising information on the issuer and on the country as a whole. A subscription agreement is

---

[96]See in general Wood, Philip, LAW AND PRACTICE OF INTERNATIONAL FINANCE, Vol. 2A, International Business & Law Series, New York, Clark Boardman Co. Ltd., 1990 (hereinafter Wood, LAW AND PRACTICE); Wilson, Nicholas, *Bond Issue Documentation*, 190–199 SOVEREIGN BORROWERS. GUIDELINES ON LEGAL NEGOTIATIONS WITH COMMERCIAL LENDERS (Lars Kalderen and Qamar S. Siddiqi editors), London, Butterworths, 1984 (hereinafter Wilson, *Bond Documentation*); and Crozer, *The Eurodollar Market*. For comparative table of syndicated loans and bond issues, see Wood, LAW AND PRACTICE, at 9–8/9–15.

[97]Wood, LAW AND PRACTICE, at 9–7.

[98]On documentation and players, see Wood, LAW AND PRACTICE, at 9–17 to 9–19; Crozer, *The Eurodollar Market*, at 68–69.

[99]Wilson, *Bond Documentation*, at 191.

entered between the issuer and the institutions in charge of managing the issue, specifying aspects related to the issue such as form, currency and denominations of the instruments, the mechanics of closing, listing, and the terms upon which the underwriters will place the bonds with investors,[100] including provisions on the selling commission and general expenses to be paid by the issuer to the managers of the transaction.

While it is not common for the structure of a bond issue involving a developing country sovereign to feature a trustee,[101] issues by private sector borrowers from developing countries have provided for intervention of a trustee who represents the universe of bondholders. Should this be the case, a trust deed is concluded specifying, among other aspects, the circumstances under which the trustee may act on behalf of the bondholders;[102] the terms and conditions of the instruments are often contained in the trust deed as well.

A fiscal agency agreement is concluded between the issuer and a financial institution in charge of making interest and principal payments to the bondholders, specifying the mechanics thereof.[103] Finally, documentation comprises the bonds themselves, a printed document upon which the terms and conditions of the instruments are reproduced.

The summary description of bond documentation undertaken above applies, as a general matter, to bonds issued in connection with debt restructuring agreements as well, with the *caveat* that, in the context of restructuring, exchange agreements replace the subscription agreements entered under fresh bond issues.

From the point of view of creditors, bonds are perceived to have a *de facto* seniority that turn them into a more attractive asset. It is believed that debtors seldom default on their bond obligations, even while incurring interest arrearages on their

[100]Wood, LAW AND PRACTICE, at 9–18.
[101]Wood, LAW AND PRACTICE, at 9–116/117: 'Sovereign states and their political sub-divisions commonly regard monitoring by a trustee as a slight to their status: the appointment of a trustee of a sovereign bond issue is accordingly rare.'
[102]Crozer, *The Eurodollar Market*, at 69.
[103]It is usually a requirement that there is always a paying agent in the country of the currency of the bonds (to protect bondholders against transfer risks) and in one other centre. If the bonds are listed, the stock exchange will commonly require a paying agent within its jurisdiction.
Wood, LAW AND PRACTICE, at 9–19.

bank loans.[104] This is essentially explained by concerns with credit standing – in other words, fears that default on bonds will entail exclusion from the market in the future, in particular because of the standard requirement of securities regulations that prospectuses disclose the issuer's debt history.[105]

The dispersed ownership of bonds entails further difficulties to a borrower seeking to restructure its debt, for negotiations in view of restructuring the terms of outstanding indebtedness require contacting an atomized universe of creditors – as opposed to easily identifiable creditors under bank loan relationships;[106] this is particular true of bonds in bearer form, which are widely used. The fact that developing country bond issues do not traditionally provide for a trustee as agent for bondholders adds to such difficulty, in that a trustee could serve as an intermediary in negotiations between the issuer and the holders of its bonds.

The negotiability that characterizes bonds further justifies creditors' preference for bonds. Although assignments of claims were allowed under provisions contained in loan documentation, as a general matter the concern with negotiability was not foremost in a commercial bank's mind in entering into a loan agreement – unlike the case of bonds, the negotiability of which also allows a borrower to reach a wider investor base.

The belief in the seniority of bonds is questionable in light of history, which shows that at times when sovereigns relied mainly on bond issues for borrowing abroad, and their external indebtedness was accordingly evidenced mostly by debt in the form of bonds, liquidity crisis led to massive defaults – on

---

[104]Stumpf, *Overview of Techniques*, at 64–65; Cline, MOBILIZING BANK LENDING, at 14. Carreau makes a parallel with the situation under domestic law:

> (...) this privileged treatment enjoyed by debt in the form of securities would be in agreement with solutions under domestic law which grant bondholders a preferential treament *vis à vis* shareholders, for instance, in the case of bankruptcy proceedings.

Carreau, Dominique, *Le Rééchelonnement de la dette extérieure des États*, 5–48 JOURNAL DU DROIT INTERNATIONAL, vol. 1, 1985, at 18 (translation supplied; hereafter Carreau, *Rééchelonnement*. It should be noted, however, that bondholders under domestic bankruptcy proceedings would *not* normally be granted preferential treatment *vis à vis* other unsecured creditors of the relevant debtor – such as bank creditors.

[105]Wood, Philip, *Debt Priorities in Sovereign Insolvency*, 4–11 IFLR November 82 (hereinafter Wood, *Debt Priorities*), at 8.

[106]Wood, *Debt Priorities*, at 8; Carreau, *Rééchelonnement*, at 18.

the foreign-held bonds.[107] In this regard, the monitoring of the debt servicing and repayment track of LDC debtors in the context of the composition of LDC debt which formed up in the late 1980s and early 1990s – i.e., primarily obligations in bond form, will certainly be useful in testing, once more, the soundness of the belief in the seniority of bonds.[108]

The believed *de facto* seniority of bonds has to a large extent been turned into a legal feature in the context of developing country debt restructuring agreements, discussed below, which involves the exchange of commercial bank debt for bonds. The agreements in question have invariably included covenants – that is, commitments in the form of contractual provisions – on the part of the debtor restructuring country to the effect that the newly issued bonds will not be subject to restructuring in the future.[109] While developing country corporate borrowers are not in a position to agree to similar covenants, for they are always subject to government action, it is expected that their bond obligations would also be excluded from global developing country external debt restructurings.

---

[107]The low degree of defaults on bonds from the middle of the 1970s on is certainly easy to understand in light of the composition of LDC external borrowing then, in which bond debt was a relatively negligible portion of the total external indebtedness. Conversely, when in the past debt took predominantly the form of bond debt, default came in the form of bond default. See Borchard, STATE INSOLVENCY. See Serbian Loans Case, PCIJ International Collection of Judgments, Series A, n. 14 (1928–1930), p. 32.

[108]This seniority may prove to mean literally what the word says: bond debt can only be *senior* to debt in the form of loan agreements; when the latter does not exist in material amounts, and bond debt prevails, seniority loses its relative nature, and bond debt becomes the main universe of restructurable obligations. Difficulties related to external indebtedness in Venezuela, Mexico and Argentina in late 1994 and early 1995 seem to provide early evidence of this point.

[109]Buchheit, Lee C., *Overview of Four Debt Reduction Programs: Mexico, Costa Rica, the Philippines and Venezuela* 77–86 LATIN AMERICAN SOVEREIGN DEBT MANAGEMENT, LEGAL AND REGULATORY ASPECTS, at 82.

The Bond Exchange Agreement entered between Brazil and its commercial bank creditors, dated September 10, 1992, contained a covenant to that effect, termed 'exit undertaking'. Section 7.01 of the agreement provides:

Section 7.01. *Covenants of Brazil*. Brazil agrees with each Purchaser that:
(. . .)
(c) Exit Undertaking. Brazil shall ensure that neither the IDU Bonds nor the IDU or ICA shall be considered part of the base amount with respect to any future request by Banco Central or Brazil for new money, and the IDU Bonds will be exempt from and not be subject to any present or future restructuring.

The agreement, discussed in Chap. 6, of this study, cleared interest arrears. The acronyms refer to 'interest due and unpaid' and 'interest on cash amount'.

It is questionable, however, to what extent the generalized inclusion of covenants related to the non-restructurable nature of the bonds in which they are contained would be an effective deterrent to a country undergoing a severe foreign exchange shortage and seeking to restructure its external indebtedness. The crisis of the 1980s demonstrated that legal commitments do not provide much comfort in face of an acute liquidity crisis. A generalization of such covenants in international bond issues by developing country borrowers might lend stronger *credibility* to the belief in the seniority of bonds, although it will probably do little to effectively turn bonds into non-restructurable instruments.

It should be noted, in any case, that the believed non-restructurable nature of bonds does not in itself make these instruments unfit for the inclusion of *contractually foreseen* adaptation provisions, as those discussed in this study. It simply means that claims evidenced by bonds are less likely to be included in an involuntary – from the viewpoint of creditors – restructuring process than claims under loan agreements.

Loan agreements excluded from this study

The analysis of adaptation of developing country borrowers' obligations under loan agreements and bond issues undertaken in this study will exclude three categories of financing transactions which, combined make up an important percentage of resource flows to developing countries. These are loans concluded with multilateral development banks; officially supported export credits; and bilateral official loans extended in the context of industrialized countries' official development assistance (ODA). Such categories of development financing transactions will be briefly reviewed in this section.

It will be mentioned in passing that financial transactions entered into between developing countries and the International Monetary Fund fall outside the scope of this study due to the fact that they do not bear the legal nature of loan agreements.[110]

[110]The official understanding of the international Monetary Fund is that IMF transactions are not loan agreeements *stricto sensu*, and its operations are not, technically speaking, development financing, but rather balance of payments assistance. See Gold, Joseph, THE LEGAL CHARACTER OF THE FUND'S STAND-BY ARRANGEMENTS AND WHY IT MATTERS, IMF Pamphlet Series, no. 35. Washington DC, IMF, 1980, 53p.

As was the case with multilateral development banks, discussed below, the IMF enjoyed a 'preferred creditor' status during the course of the debt crisis of the 1980s, and developing country members maintained their financial obligations towards the institution outside the scope of debt restructuring agreements.[111]

Multilateral development bank loans

The International Bank for Reconstruction and Development (IBRD), or World Bank, and the regional development banks established and modeled on it – the Inter-American Development Bank, the Asian Development Bank, the African Development Bank and the European Bank for Reconstruction and Development – are multilateral institutions established by intergovernmental treaties with the purpose of financing development. While they carry out the developmental purpose for which they were set up in a number of ways, loan agreements entered with borrowers in their developing member countries constitute the main thrust of their activities.[112]

Developing country external indebtedness towards multilateral development banks was excluded from adaptation through restructuring exercises in the course of the debt crisis of the 1980s, even while debt owed to private sector and official creditors was

---

According to Petersmann, 'from a legal point of view, the Fund's financial assistance is provided in the form of "currency sales" to its members, or "purchases" of foreign currency by the member, to be followed by a "repurchase" of the same amount of currency by the Fund after a specified period of time', Petersmann, FINANCIAL ASSISTANCE, at 25.

IMF operations will only be discussed in this study to the extent they are useful or necessary to the understanding of issues related to syndicated bank loans or bond issues.

[111]On the preferred creditor status of the IMF, see Martha, Rutsel Silvester J., *Preferred Creditor Status under International Law: The Case of the International Monetary Fund*, 801–826 ICLQ, vol. 39 (1990).

[112]For an overview of the World Bank's activities, see Mason, Edward S., and Asher, Robert E., THE WORLD BANK SINCE BRETTON WOODS, Washington DC, Brookings Institution, 1979, 915p.; Broches, Aron, *The World Bank*, 83–96, 2 INTERNATIONAL FINANCIAL LAW. LENDING, CAPITAL TRANSFERS AND INSTITUTIONS (Robert S. Rendell editor), London, Euromoney, 2nd edition 1984; on the European Bank for Reconstruction and Development, see Shihata, Ibrahim, *The Role of the European Bank for Reconstruction and Development in the Promotion and Financing of Investment in Central and Eastern Europe: A Legal Analysis*, 207–231 ICSID REVIEW – FOREIGN INVESTMENT LAW JOURNAL vol. 5, fall 1990.

restructured in a systematic manner.[113] Such 'preferred creditor' status enjoyed by multilateral development institutions is somewhat in contrast with provisions written into their constitutive instruments which enable them to agree to measures adapting the obligations of borrowers undergoing financial difficulties.

The Articles of Agreement of the World Bank provide that the Bank may, under particular circumstances, 'modify the terms of amortization', 'extend the life of a loan' or 'accept service repayment on the loan in the member's currency', if the borrowing member country is suffering from an 'acute currency stringency'.[114] In case of actual default, the Articles of Agreement provide that '[the Bank] shall make such arrangements as may be feasible to adjust the obligations under the loans'.[115] Such modalities of adaptation envisaged in the Bank's Charter, had they been undertaken, would have recalled the main features of debt restructuring agreements concluded in the course of the debt crisis between developing countries and private sector creditors, and surveyed later in this study.

Like those of the World Bank, the constitutive instruments of the regional development banks contain provisions which would in principle allow for some relaxation of borrowers' obligations, even though none go into as much detail as do the IBRD Articles. Article VII, Section 3 of the Articles of Agreement of the Inter-American Development Bank[116] and Article 18 of the Asian

[113]The European Bank for Reconstruction and Development is an exception from this 'preferred creditor' experience, since it was not established until 1990, and had no credits outstanding at the time the crisis evolved.

World Bank loans were adapted in several instances, but on project grounds, not due to financial difficulties experienced by a developing country borrower. See Asser, Tobias M.C., *The World Bank and the Renegotiation and Adaptation of Long-Term Loans*, 253–269 ADAPTATION AND RENEGOTIATION OF CONTRACTS IN INTERNATIONAL TRADE AND FINANCE (Norbert Horn editor), Antwerp, Kluwer, 1985, 421p.

[114]Article IV, Section 4(c) of the Articles of Agreement of the World Bank, dated December 27, 1945, 2 UNTS 134.

[115]Article IV, 7 of the Articles of Agreement of the World Bank. The latter possibility – payment in local currency – bears a parallel with 'dollar constraint' provisions included in bond documentation relating to developing country corporate borrowers, as briefly reviewed in Chap. 6 of this study.

[116]April 4, 1959; 389 UNTS 69:

(Article VII) Section 3. Methods of Meeting Liabilities of the Bank in Case of Defaults

(a) The Bank, in the event of actual or threatened default on loans made or guaranteed by the Bank using its ordinary capital resources, shall take such action as it deems appropriate with respect to modifying the terms of the loan, other than the currency of repayment.

Development Bank[117] authorize the Banks to take such action as they deem appropriate, even though solely upon actual default on the part of a borrower; so do the Articles of Agreement of the latest development bank, the European Bank for Reconstruction and Development, albeit in a somewhat mild manner.[118] The only exception in this regard is the African Development Bank, the charter of which does not contain a provision to that effect.[119]

The 'preferred creditor' status enjoyed by the World Bank and other multilateral financial institutions does not rest upon any norm of international law or on any formal convention between creditors, for there exist none to that effect.[120] Instead, the con-

---

[117]December 4, 1965; 571 UNTS 123:

Article 18. Methods of Meeting Liabilities of the Bank
1. In case of defaults on loans made, participated in or guaranteed by the Bank in its ordinary operations, the Bank shall take such action as it deems appropriate with respect to modifying the terms of the loan, other than the currency of repayment.

[118]The Articles of Agreement of the EBRD, entered on May 29, 1990, are reproduced in ICSID REVIEW – FOREIGN INVESTMENT LAW JOURNAL vol. 5, n. 2, fall. 90, p. 326:

Article 17. Methods of Meeting the Losses of the Bank.
1. In the Bank's ordinary operations, in cases of arrears or default on loans made, participated in, or guaranteed by the Bank, and in cases of losses on underwriting and in equity investment, the Bank shall take such action as it deems appropriate.

Comparing the provisions of the Articles of Agreement of the EBRD with those of the IBRD, the General Counsel of the latter notes, in regard to the issue of adaptation, that '[the EBRD] Agreement avoids similar provisions in its text'. Shihata, Ibrahim, THE EUROPEAN BANK FOR RECONSTRUCTION AND DEVELOPMENT. A COMPARATIVE ANALYSIS OF THE CONSTITUENT AGREEMENT, London/Dordrecht/Boston, Martinus Nijhoff, 1990, 189p., at 73.

[119]Instead, the charter of the AfDB (510 UNTS 3) provides for a mechanism which has the Bank recompose its capital in case of default. Article 21 (*Methods of Meeting Liabilities of the Bank*) provides:

(2) In case of default in respect of a loan made out of borrowed funds or guaranteed by the Bank as part of its ordinary operations, the Bank may, if it believes that the default may be of long duration, call an additional amount of such callable capital not to exceed in any one year one percent of the total subscriptions of the members, for the following purposes:
(a) To redeem before maturity, or otherwise discharge, its liability on all or part of the outstanding principal of any loan guaranteed by it in respect of which the debtor is in default; and
(b) To repurchase, or otherwise discharge, its liability on all or part of its own outstanding borrowing.

[120]A survey of loan documentation related to sovereign debt restructuring reveals an indirect acknowledgment of the World Bank's preferred creditor status. In

certed debt strategy that was adopted in the course of the debt crisis entailed exclusion of multilateral debt from restructuring agreements on the basis of financial and economic considerations.

The financial terms of loan agreements concluded between developing country borrowers and multilateral development banks reflect the terms such banks obtain themselves under their borrowing transactions.[121] Thus, borrowers can obtain financial terms which are more favorable than they could otherwise obtain on a commercial basis. There is a perception that development banks' agreeing to restructuring their claims would undermine their credit standing in international financial markets from which they borrow through the issuing of bonds, and where they are rated as prime credit, thus ultimately affecting the terms on which they on-lend.[122]

In addition, multilateral banks primarily provide project financing, as opposed to general purpose lending. There is a perception that project lending should be excluded from sover-

---

particular, World Bank loans – as well as obligations towards the IMF and the Bank for International Settlements – were often expressly designated within the category of external indebtedness of the restructuring country excluded from restructuring exercises; they may be excluded from the purview of *mandatory prepayment* provisions as well.

Carreau submits that the practice of excluding credits of multilateral institutions from restructuring exercises amounts to a 'custom':

> (. . .) the credits of intergovernmental organizations enjoy a privileged treatment in the sense that they must always be honored and serviced according to the agreed payment schedule. One would search in vain for a contract provision establishing such a principle. (. . .) It would not be improper to consider that this treatment granted to international intergovernmental institutions has customary value (. . .)

Carreau, Dominique, *Rééchelonnement* at 14–15 (translation supplied).

[121]With respect to the terms of World Bank lending transactions, see Broches, Aron, *The World Bank*, 83–96, 2 INTERNATIONAL FINANCIAL LAW. LENDING, CAPITAL TRANSFERS AND INSTITUTIONS (Robert S. Rendell editor), London, Euromoney, 2nd edition 1984, at 89.

[122]On the credit rating of the World Bank, see in general Parker, Cheryl. THE WORLD BANK: A CRITICAL ANALYSIS. New York, Monthly Press Review, 1982, 414p. (hereinafter Parker, BANK CRITICAL ANALYSIS), at 44.

On the likely impact of the World Bank's participating in developing country debt restructuring exercises, see *Hearings before the Subcommittee on International Development Institutions and Finance of the Committee on Banking, Finance and Urban Affairs of the House of Representatives* 245, 245–246 9 (hereinafter *Hearings*) Serial No. 100–62, 1988; and in particular Testimony of S. Melvin Rines, Managing Director of the investment firm Kidder, Peabody, on May 11, 1988, reproduced in Appendix of the *Hearings*.

eign debt restructuring as a matter of principle due to the rationale of project lending: unlike general purpose lending, project financing is supposed to permit the parties to the loan agreement to match debt service obligations to the cash flow of the productive investment being financed.[123] In this regard, exclusion from reorganization is supposed to work as a precondition to preserving the link between the loan and the project's revenue generating capacity.[124]

There is much to be said in favor of safeguarding the credit standing of multilateral development banks, the institutional objectives of which are to foster development through the provision of financing on conditions not readily accessible to its developing country members in the market-place. However, in light of the express provisions of the constitutive instruments of such institutions, it is awkward that multilateral development banks' credits should be altogether exempted from restructuring in the context of a generalized debt crisis, as they were in the 1980s.[125] The erecting of any such policy into an absolute principle runs contrary to the institutional objective of the institutions, and indeed to the intent of their founders.[126]

---

[123]See Stockmayer, Albrecht, *Excluding Project Loans from Sovereign Reschedulings*, IFLR March 1985 (hereinafter Stockmayer, *Excluding Project Loans*), at 26.
[124]Stockmayer, *Excluding Project Loans*, at 26.
[125]The World Bank's general policy of non-rescheduling is publicized in materials related to the Bank's borrowing activities and in its annual reports. Recent developments regarding the World Bank's treatment of protracted arrears would seem to suggest that there may be a shift in the Bank's policy regarding the adaptation of the obligations of a borrower which is undergoing protracted financial difficulties. Under such changed policy, the terms of a Bank loan may be adjusted so as to reflect the softer terms of the Bank's sister institution, the International Development Association (established on September 24, 1960; 439 UNTS 250). Interview with Executive Director of the World Bank, March 1993.
[126]On June 9, 1944, eve of the Bretton Woods Conference at which the World Bank and the International Monetary Fund were established, Lord Keynes, head of the British delegation to the Conference and one of the fathers of both institutions, wrote in a note dated to T. Padmore, Private Secretary to the Chancellor of the Exchequer:

The Planning of International Investment
It should be a primary duty of the Bank to secure that investment is not made haphazard, but that the more useful schemes are dealt with first; also to co-ordinate investment, whether it is made or guaranteed by the Bank, or made otherwise; and in short to see that international lending is a more wisely conceived plan than it was after the last war, and is not the ill-conceived racket that it was on that occasion. It would also be the duty of the Bank to consider carefully the capacity of borrowing countries to meet the service of the loans, and to take pains not to make loans except where there

Officially supported export credits and official bilateral loans

Export credits and bilateral official loans, although extended under concessional terms, as described in the following, have been 'adapted' *de facto* in the context of the debt problem of developing countries under the aegis of the 'Paris Club', which is the forum for official debt restructuring.[127]

Export credits are loans extended to importers to allow them to defer payment for purchases made. Governments' involvement in providing export finance can take different forms. Official support to export finance can constitute *direct financial support*. This can take the form of direct export credits extended by the government agency; of refinancing of a portion of credits extended by private institutions; or of subsidizing the difference between the market interest rate at which the lending private institution itself borrows, and the lower fixed rates at which it extends the credit.[128]

Alternatively, export agencies can limit themselves to providing 'pure cover' – that is to say, guarantees or insurance to

---

is a position to develop after having received the loan, an adequate favorable balance to meet the service.

On the other hand a loan once having been made, if the borrowing country is in difficulties about the service of the loan, for reasons beyond its own control, it should be the duty of the Bank to help it to retrieve its position and not to impose any penalties, except where the borrowing country is at fault. In particular, the Bank should accept local currency in paper for a limited period.

THE COLLECTED WRITINGS OF JOHN MAYNARD KEYNES, vol. 25, ACTIVITIES 1940–1944: SHAPING THE POST-WAR WORLD: THE CLEARING UNION (D. Moggridge editor), 1990, at 52–53.

[127]See Camdessus, Michel, *Government Creditors and the Role of the Paris Club*, 125–130 DEFAULT AND RESCHEDULING: CORPORATE AND SOVEREIGN BORROWERS (David Suratgar editor), London, Euromoney, 1984, 163p.; Carreau, *Rééchelonnement*, at 18–26; Hardy, Chandra S., RESCHUDULING DEVELOPING COUNTRY DEBTS, 1956–1981: LESSONS AND RECOMMENDATIONS, Washington DC, Overseas Development Council, June 1982, Monograph no. 15, 74p.; Hudes, Karen, *Coordination of Paris and London Club Reschedulings*, 553–571 NEW YORK JOURNAL OF INTERNATIONAL LAW AND POLICY, vol. 17 (1985); Rieffel, Alexis, *The Paris Club, 1978–1983*, 83–110 COLUMBIA JOURNAL OF TRANSNATIONAL LAW vol. 23 (1984); Rieffel, Alexis, *The Role of the Paris Club in Managing Debt Problems*, Essays in International Finance no. 161. Princeton, Princeton University, December 1985, 38p.; and the IMF publications, periodically updated, *Multilateral Official Debt Rescheduling. Recent Experience*, Washington DC, IMF.

[128]Cizauskas, Albert C., *The Changing Nature of Export Credit Finance and its Implications for Developing Countries*, World Bank Working Paper no. 409, Washington DC, World Bank, July 1980, 28p. (hereinafter Cizauskas, *The Changing Nature*), at 7.

direct financing extended by a third party.[129] All major industrialized countries, and some developing countries as well, have established systems to encourage the extending of export credit, either in the form of direct finance or guarantee/insurance cover.[130]

Officially supported export credits are extended on somewhat similar terms across borders due to the existence of international institutional arrangements designed to impose some discipline to the field, and thus avoid 'export credit wars' fought to assure export markets. Also, industrialized countries have been attempting to bring export credits loans to terms closer to those existing under market conditions.[131]

In 1976, at the seventh annual summit meeting of the most industrialized nations, a non-binding set of guidelines was agreed upon, stipulating minimum down payments and interest rates as well as a maximum duration of credits; this set of guidelines was named the 'Consensus'. In 1978, the Consensus was enlarged by the OECD member countries in a document called the 'Arrangement on Guidelines for Officially Supported Export Credits'. This Arrangement, as subsequently amended, is the document that currently sets minimum standards to which

[129]THE EXPORT CREDIT FINANCING SYSTEMS IN OECD COUNTRIES, Paris, OECD, 3rd edition, 1987 (hereinafter EXPORT CREDIT SYSTEMS), at 7.

[130]The organizational form of government involvement in export finance differs widely. The institution providing finance or guarantee – the export credit agency – can be a department within a ministry, an autonomous agency within the administrative structure, or a private institutional operating in accordance with government instructions. See EXPORT CREDIT SYSTEMS, at 9; Dillon, K. Burke, Duran-Downing, Luis, and Xafa, Miranda, OFFICIALLY SUPPORTED EXPORT CREDITS. DEVELOPMENT AND PROSPECTS, World Economic and Financial Surveys, Washington DC, IMF, February 1988, 47p. (hereinafter EXPORT CREDITS February 1988), footnote 1 at 1.

These differing institutional arrangements are also reflected in funding arrangements: export agencies can be funded through direct budgetary appropriations, special government funds, loans and capital from the government, or shares and bonds, in the case of private institutions; EXPORT CREDIT SYSTEMS, at 9.

[131]The 1990 edition of the IMF survey on export credits stated:

Agencies said that the days when governments were prepared to spend large sums on export promotion are clearly gone. Moreover, the idea that official lending to sovereign borrowers is risk-free no longer holds. Agencies, particularly those in Europe that pioneered the techniques of export credit insurance, are undergoing a challenging period of transition. Over time, the scope of nonmarket competition for exports is likely to continue to decline, and agencies' response to these challenges will determine the role they will play in international capital flows in the 1990s.

EXPORT CREDITS May 1990, at 2.

official support to export is to conform.[132] Although the Arrangement does not specifically regulate 'pure cover' – that is to say, insurance and guarantee of export credits – it does apply to conditions and terms of export credits to which some sort of officially supported cover is attached.

The OECD Arrangement is built upon four main elements, or requirements, concerning the extension of officially supported credit.[133] These are a minimum cash down payment of 15 percent of the export contract value; maximum repayment periods; minimum interest rates; and a minimum grant element for mixed credits, that is to say, financing in which export credit is combined with official aid grants.[134]

In establishing minimum interest rates, as well as maximum repayment periods, the Arrangement divided recipient countries into three categories – relatively rich, intermediate and relatively poor countries, the dividing criterion being essentially per capita income.[135] Maximum repayment term is eight and a half years, extendable to ten years in the case of relatively poor countries; principal repayment is made in equal semi-annual installments beginning no later than six months after the starting point of the contract.[136] Minimum interest rates are determined in accordance

---

[132]The text of the Arrangement is reproduced in EXPORT CREDIT SYSTEMS, at 265.
[133]Johnson, G.G., Fisher, Matthew, and Harris, Elliott, OFFICIALLY SUPPORTED EXPORT CREDITS. DEVELOPMENTS AND PROSPECTS, World Economic and Financial Surveys, Washington DC, IMF, May 1990 (hereinafter EXPORT CREDITS May 1990). Appendix IV, at 38: *The OECD Consensus on Export Credits.*
[134]The use of mixed credits has the effect of enhancing the attractiveness of the export finance offered, by making it less costly for the borrower/importer. By imposing a minimum grant element in mixed credits, the Arrangement seeks to render more transparent this disguised type of export promotion instrument.
[135]Since July 1982, category I comprises all countries with a per capita gross domestic product of over $4,000 per annum; category III countries, as all those eligible for IDA credits as well as any low-income countries or territories whose GNP per capita would not exceed the IDA eligibility level; and category II, all remaining countries. EXPORT CREDITS May 1990, Appendix IV, at 39.
[136]EXPORT CREDITS May 1990, Appendix IV, at 38.
The 'starting point' of the contract is the point in time when the importer receives delivery of the financed goods or takes possession of a completed plant. This implies a grace period in the financing, namely that between the signing of the export contract and the delivery of the goods, equivalent to the manufacturing period. Export credits do not carry explicit grace periods. *The Changing Nature*, at 15.

with a 'uniform moving matrix', which is adjusted biannually.[137] Due to marked competition for export markets, the *minimum* interest rates established by the Arrangement are in fact *maximum* rates.[138]

Official development assistance

Official development assistance (ODA)[139] of industrialized countries can take the form of loans or outright grants to developing countries, and can be provided either bilaterally, usually by an official bilateral aid agency, or multilaterally, though contributions to multilateral development institutions such as the World Bank and the regional development banks.[140]

Although there are significant differences among individual countries,[141] the major industrial countries, under the umbrella of the Development Assistance Committee (DAC) of the Organization for Economic Cooperation and Development (OECD), try to achieve a certain uniformity in the financial terms of grants and loans extended under official development assistance. Ideally, countries' assistance should conform to the *Recommenda-*

[137]The Arrangement also includes a monthly-adjustable 'commercial interest reference rates' (CIRR) matrix, to avoid placing credits denominated in low-interest rate currencies at a competitive disadvantage. EXPORT CREDITS May 1990, Appendix IV, at 39.

[138]*The Changing Nature*, at 8; Frenkel, Orit, and Fontheim, Claude G.B., *Export Credits: An International and Domestic Legal Analysis*, 1069–1088 LAW & POLICY INTERNATIONAL BUSINESS vol. 13 (1981), at 1074.

[139]ODA, as defined by the Development Assistance Committee (DAC) of the Organization for Economic Cooperation and Development (OECD), 'consists of grants and loans to developing countries, provided either bilaterally or multilaterally, that are undertaken by the public sector, have the promotion of economic development and welfare as their main objectives, and are offered on concessional financial terms', AID FOR DEVELOPMENT: THE KEY ISSUES. SUPPORTING MATERIALS FOR THE REPORT OF THE TASK FORCE ON CONCESSIONAL FLOWS, Washington DC, IMF/World Bank Development Committee, 1986, 138p. (hereinafter, AID FOR DEVELOPMENT), at 4.

[140]In fact, the largest single source of development assistance is the International Development Association (IDA) of the World Bank Group. Other sources include the soft loan windows of the Inter-American Development Bank, of the African Development Bank, and of the Asian Development Bank; the European Development Fund, which is the concessional aid agency of the European Economic Community, the Arab Fund for Social and Economic Development, and the OPEC Fund. AID FOR DEVELOPMENT, at 9–10. For a picture of ODA from non-DAC Sources, see the annual OECD reports, *Development Cooperation*.

[141]See section on *Trends in AID from Individual DAC Members in Development Cooperation*, 1990 Report. Paris, OECD, 272p., at 137–153.

tion on Terms and Conditions of Aid.[142] The *Recommendation* establishes a single target of an 86 percent grant element[143] for the members' annual ODA program – grants and loans included – with a subtarget of 90 percent in the case of assistance to the least developed countries.[144]

[142]The current version of this document was adopted by the DAC in 1978. *Recommendations on Terms and Conditions of Aid*, adopted by the Development Assistance Committee on February 28, 1978, with Italy having reserved its position. Annex III of Development Cooperation Report 1988.
[143]'In order to achieve a further softening of overall financial terms of ODA, Members should endeavour fully to maintain or achieve as soon as possbile an average grant element in their ODA commitments of at least 86%', Section 2 of the *Recommendations*.
The 'grant element is defined as 'a composite measure of the financial terms of a transaction, giving in one figure the combined concessionality of the interest rate, maturity and grace period of a loan. A grant element arises when the interest rate charged is lower than the discount rate. The discount rate of ten percent used by the DAC for calculating the grant element of ODA is supposed to reflect broadly the donor's opportunity cost of capital. It is a largely conventional figure which does not reflect the often substantial differences in interest levels among donor countries nor changes over time.'
Development Cooperation, 1987 Report, Paris, OECD, 263p., at 110.
[144]Section 8 of the *Recommendations* provides that:

> Official Development Assistance to these [least-developed] countries should be essentially in the form of grants and, as a minimum, the average grant element of all commitments from a given donor should either be at least 86 percent to each Least-Developed Country over a period of three years, or at least 90 percent annually for the Least-Developed countries as a group.

Chapter Three

AD HOC ADAPTATION AND THE DEBT CRISIS OF THE 1980s

Borrowers and their creditors coped with the debt crisis of the 1980s by entering a series of restructuring agreements, in a process which amounted to *ad hoc* contract adaptation. The modification of borrowers' obligations which the conclusion of restructuring agreements entailed amounts to agreed adaptation of contractual terms.

In the following, the patterns of contract adaptation arising out of the successive restructuring agreements will be analyzed. Beforehand, the reasons for lenders and borrowers opting for renegotiation rather than litigation will be briefly sketched.

Avoiding litigation

The debt crisis of the 1980s brought about a disruption of the multitude of outstanding loan agreements, with borrowers failing to fulfill their obligations to repay principal and/or service interest. Such disruption could conceivably have led to a large-scale process of litigation. Creditors would have had an obvious case to make, in that there was manifest failure on the part of debtors to perform their contractual obligations. Borrowers, too, could conceivably have sought judicial relief from performance.

Creditors could have exercised the remedies provided under the agreements in case of an event of default, including the rights to declare the loans immediately due and payable and to cancel any commitments to make further disbursements.[145] In order to collect the sums owed by a debtor, however, creditors would have had to sue for repayment. The path of litigation was not

---

[145]See Wood, INTERNATIONAL FINANCE, at 170.

considered a practical or satisfactory one by lenders. While such reluctance to litigate is by no means peculiar to development lending, the reasons in the particular instance of the debt crisis were manifold, and economic and practical as much as legal in nature.

Litigation would have been detrimental to the long-term relationship between each individual creditor and the relevant debtor. At the outset of the crisis, the predominant perception was that the financial difficulties of developing country debtors were part of a liquidity problem which could be overcome with time. In this context, taking the radical step of suing the debtor was deemed to be a wrong business strategy.

From a practical point of view, it was also perceived that failure to meet obligations under external indebtedness was prompted not only by unwillingness, but also by inability to pay. Creditors would have had difficulties obtaining satisfaction of a favorable judgment or arbitral award in the absence of assets of considerable value outside the jurisdiction of the debtors' own courts.

The stringent requirements imposed by the set-off rules of the governing laws would rule out pre-emptive action whereby a lender which was also a debtor under deposit agreements could effectuate automatic satisfaction of its claim.[146] In addition, deposits potentially subject to set-off would have most certainly been depleted by the debtor in question in anticipation of a move to set off by the relevant creditor.[147]

In those cases where the debtor was the sovereign or the Central Bank, statutory immunity would, absent an express waiver, impose further obstacles to the obtaining of satisfaction of a favorable judgment – assuming no immunity from suit had intervened earlier in the process – or arbitral award through attachment or execution proceedings.

Loan documentation also presented, and paradoxically so, difficulties to the exercise of creditors' rights. Sharing clauses meant that whatever payment was obtained would have to be divided on a *pro rata* basis with other creditors under the same instru-

---

[146]Among other requirements, for a bank to operate lawfully a set-off, thereby using deposits of the borrower to pay out the defaulted loan, the loan must be mature and payable; and there must be mutuality, i.e. the depositor and the debtor must be the same legal person. See Wood, INTERNATIONAL FINANCE, at 173.

[147]Semkow, *Syndicating*, at 918.

ment.[148] In addition, cross-default clauses implied that one lawsuit would automatically trigger event of default clauses under other, distinct loan agreements, possibly leading to a race to the courtroom by creditors.

Borrowers, in turn, could have conceivably presented defenses aimed at relief from contractual performance based on argument that the circumstances which prompted their failure to fulfill contractual obligations under external indebtedness amounted to exceptional circumstances beyond their control which, under the law governing the relevant agreements, could be considered an admissible excuse for non-performance, and accordingly lead to the termination or the revision of the agreements.[149] This reasoning, if put forward in the context of hypothetical litigation, would have led to judicial review of the issue of changed circumstances as excuse for non-performance under the law governing the relevant agreements,[150] which would typically be English or New York law for most, as reviewed above.

It is arguably an open question whether the particular circumstances of the debt crisis would fulfill the requirements developed under the English judicial doctrine of frustration of contract,[151] as well as the notion of commercial impracticability

[148]See Wood, INTERNATIONAL FINANCE, at 272.

[149]See, in general, Walde, Thomas, *The Sanctity of Debt and Insolvent Countries: Defenses of Debtors in International Loan Agreements*, 119–145 JUDICIAL ENFORCEMENT INTERNATIONAL DEBT OBILIGATIONS (David M. Sassoon and Daniel·D. Bradlow editors), Washington DC, International Law Institute, 1987, 173p.

[150]On contract adaptation under various domestic legal systems, see Horn, Norbert, *Changes in Circumstances and the Revision of Contracts in Some European Laws and in International Law*, 15–29 ADAPTATION AND RENEGOTIATION OF CONTRACTS IN INTERNATIONAL TRADE AND FINANCE (Norbert Horn editor), Antwerp, Kluwer, 1985, 421p. (hereinafter Horn, *Changes in Circumstances*); and Gold, Joseph, chapter on 'Hardship, Impracticability, Unconscionability, Unforeseeability', in LEGAL EFFECTS OF FLUCTUATING EXCHANGE RATES, Washington DC, IMF, 1990, 473p., at 226–247.

[151]Schmithoff points out that

English decisions show that the courts consider the principle of sanctity of contract as of infinitely higher importance than the requirements of commercial convenience and that they will not lightly assume that a contract which is still capable of performance is frustrated.

Schmithoff, Clive M., EXPORT TRADE. THE LAW AND PRACTICE OF INTERNATIONAL TRADE, London, Stevens & Sons, 9th edition 1990, 798p., at 190.

developed by courts in the United States,[152] both of which impose stringent conditions that must be met before a party can obtain leave from its contractual obligations. In particular, it is questionable whether the requirement of unforeseeability, which is common to both doctrines, would be deemed to be fulfilled in regard to the changes which characterized the debt crisis. Although the so-called debt crisis was prompted by a set of external shocks, at least with regard to interest rate fluctuations, counsels for creditors would certainly argue, and probably rightly so, that such variations were not unforeseeable, given the floating interest rates structure of the relevant loan agreements.

Litigation was thus considered unsatisfactory for lenders and debtors alike. This is evidenced by the extremely meager litigation that arose in connection with the debt crisis.[153] The path chosen by borrowers and creditors was to renegotiate the terms of the contracts, by concluding restructuring agreements. In so proceeding, rather than relying on contract provisions regarding remedies against default, or on statutes or judicial doctrines related to changes in circumstances, debtors and creditors relied on the general principle of contract law according to which parties have autonomy to conclude those agreements which best suit their interests.

The debt strategy: ad hoc *adaptation*

The composition of developing country external indebtedness at the time the crisis erupted was complex. The external debt profile of restructuring countries revealed both public as well as private sector debtors, in addition to the sovereign itself, while creditors included a multitude of private sector banks from all major

---

[152]Section 2–615 of the United States Uniform Commercial Code provides:

Except so far as the seller may have assumed a greater obligation (. . .) a non-delivery (. . .) is not a breach of (. . .) duty if performance as agreed has been made impracticable by the occurrence of a contingency the non-occurrence of which was a basic assumption on which the contract was made.

On the question of adaptation under US law, see Buxbaum, Richard, *Modification and Adaptation: American Developments*, 31–54 ADAPTATION AND RENEGOTIATION OF CONTRACTS IN INTERNATIONAL TRADE AND FINANCE (Norbert Horn editor), Antwerp, Kluwer, 1985, 421p.

[153]See Bhandari, Jagdeep S., *International Debt Litigation in United States Courts*, 383–421 GERMAN YEARBOOK OF INTERNATIONAL LAW, vol. 33 (1990).

industrial countries, usually organized in large syndicates. The nature of the credits involved also showed a great diversity: general purpose loans, project finance, export credits, interbank trade lines; typically, only the former were included in the restructuring exercise.[154]

Different debtors negotiated with different groups of creditor banks, and each group was moved by different incentives as well as inhibited by particular constraints, such as differing regulatory environments, levels of exposure to particular countries, varying accounting practices and financial reporting requirements.[155]

Despite this impressive diversity of elements, however, the pattern of contract adaptation which arose from the developing country debt restructuring agreements was characterized by a marked uniformity, and a 'debt strategy' was adopted by the players involved – the developing country debtors, their commercial bank creditors, and also the official sector, to the extent it was called upon to help put together financing packages or to serve as mediator when negotiations became stalled.

The main features of debt restructuring agreements evolved and changed as initial expectations as to the nature and duration of the crisis had to be reviewed, with renewed restructuring packages for the same debtors being required. A diversification of the instruments used in debt adjustment came about, and the 'menu approach' which characterized the latest phase of the debt negotiations took over.

The following section examines the pattern of contract adaptation that underlay the successive phases of the crisis.

The initial phase

As noted earlier, the debt restructuring agreements concluded in the initial phase of the debt crisis reflected the then predominant belief that developing country debtors' inability to pay interest and principal on external indebtedness was the result of a temporary liquidity problem, which could be overcome with the

[154]Debts owed to official creditors, and renegotiated in the Paris Club, will not be included in the following analysis. For a brief discussion and references on 'official' debts, see the introductory part of this study.
[155]See Mudge, Alfred, *Sovereign Debt Restructuring: A Current Perspective*, 85–90 DEFAULT AND RESCHEDULING. CORPORATE AND SOVEREIGN BORROWERS IN DIFFICULTY (David Suratgar editor), London, Euromoney, 1984, 163p. (hereinafter Mudge, *Sovereign Debt Restructuring*), at 85.

adoption of internal adjustment measures. It followed from this perception that the appropriate course of action consisted in providing debtors with temporary financial relief. This translated into the rescheduling of principal maturities falling due in the short run, coupled with the provision of financing to allow for debtors to maintain current interest service. This factor was essential in avoiding the need to declare a formal default, as well as in upholding banks' apparent financial soundness.[156]

As a counterpart to these financial arrangements, the debtor committed itself to undertake economic adjustment measures designed to redress its external imbalances and ultimately enable it to resume regular payment of interest and principal. These adjustment programs were typically monitored by the International Monetary Fund.

Negotiations were carried out between authorities of the debtor country and a group of banks representing the country's largest creditors – the 'bank advisory group', or 'steering committee'.[157] The initial debt strategy thus relied on three basic pillars: rescheduling, refinancing and IMF-monitored economic policy adjustment.

Rescheduling   Rescheduling in a strict sense amounts to deferring principal installments of the specified types of debt falling due within a certain period to a later date.[158] In the initial phase of the crisis, only payments of principal installments falling due on the current, or at most on the two first years ensuing the restructuring plan, were deferred. The practice was subsequently

[156][by] stretching maturities over a long period, a debt which clearly cannot be paid in the short term becomes a debt which may be paid in the long-term. At least the problem is deferred, and the banks' books may appear healthier from a financial and regulatory point of view.'

Wickersham, Warren G., *Problems of Documentation in Rescheduling of Sovereign Bank Debt*, 117–123 DEFAULT AND RESCHEDULING. CORPORATE AND SOVEREIGN BORROWERS IN DIFFICULTY (David Suratgar editor), London, Euromoney, 1984, 163p., at 118.

[157]For a description of 'bank advisory committees' in the context of sovereign debt restructuring, see Mudge, Alfred, *Sovereign Debt Restructure: A Perspective of Counsel to Agent Banks, Bank Advisory Groups and Servicing Banks*, 59–74 COLUMBIA JOURNAL OF TRANSNATIONAL LAW vol. 23 (1984) (hereinafter Mudge, *Perspective of Counsel*), in particular at 65–72.

[158]Not all external indebtedness was included in the restructuring package. Arrangements are typically made for the maintenance of interbank lines of credit and of short-term trade lines of credit.

altered, and the pattern became the conclusion of multi-year rescheduling agreements, whereby principal falling due on a number of years from the initial date would be rescheduled. Multi-year reschedulings provided debtor countries with a less stringent time-frame to plan and implement adjustments, while reducing the imminence of repayment pressures.[159]

Documentation issues in the rescheduling arrangements were made complex by the existence of myriad loan agreements, syndicated or not, which evidenced a debtor country's overall outstanding indebtedness at a particular point in time. Nevertheless, clear patterns in documentation arose.[160] While a large number and wide diversity of agreements were concluded, restructuring packages would typically take the form of either 'umbrella' rescheduling agreements, which would later translate into implementing agreements; or of deposit schemes.

A first rescheduling method thus consisted in having an agreement in principle function as an 'umbrella' agreement, with subsequent changes reported to the individual original loan agreements.[161] The restructuring agreement would be concise and limited to providing for the modifications to be inserted in the original agreements. The arrangement would not amount to a novation[162] of the contracts, through substitution of the parties to the agreement, or through a modification of the terms, financial or otherwise, of the outstanding contractual arrangements. The original loan agreements would remain in force, and would incorporate the changes agreed upon in the negotiations

[159]Bergstein, BANK LENDING, at 36.
[160]As described by one attorney active in the process:

> Although the specifics have varied from country to country, the essence of the restructure process has been the same. It has been a continuing revision of the contractual IOU: I owe you X amount in Y currency on Z date. Debt restructuring has been nothing more than changing this formula by contractual agreement of many parties – changing the X, the Y and the Z and, in some cases, also changing the obligor and the interest rate.

Mudge, Alfred, *Country Debt Restructure, 1982–1987: An Overview*, 141–146 CURRENT LEGAL ISSUES AFFECTING CENTRAL BANKS (Robert C. Effros editor), Washington DC, International Monetary Fund, 1992, vol. 1, 642p. at 145.
[161]This method bears a clear parallel with official debt restructuring under the auspices of the Paris Club, as noted by Mudge, Alfred, *Sovereign Debt Restructuring*, at 90.
[162]In the sense of civil law, which may amount to substitution by mutual agreement of one debtor for another or of one creditor for another; but also to substitution of a new debt for the old one. BLACK'S LAW DICTIONARY, abridged 6th edition, 1991.

regarding, for instance, maturity schedule, including grace periods, and spread over interest rate.

In terms of contract adaptation, the operation would amount to an amendment to the terms of the contract by virtue of a subsequent agreement between the parties, even though not all lenders, or syndicates of lenders, participated directly in the negotiations leading to the amendment: instead, they were represented, under a somewhat informal arrangement, by the steering committee. The acts of this committee did not create legal rights or obligations;[163] the contractual modifications would not take effect unless ultimately agreed upon by the creditor under the original loan agreement.

Under a second method of debt restructuring, the arrangement between the debtor and the bank advisory committee would provide that the Central Bank of the debtor country establish a foreign currency deposit in favor of the foreign creditors. The agreement would provide that the borrowers under the original loan agreements make payments, as they became due, in local currency into the Central Bank account denominated in local currency. Deposits from individual debtors were consolidated into one single deposit facility, with the Central Bank replacing the original borrowers as obligor under the new credit agreement and committing to credit corresponding amounts in foreign currency in favor of the original lenders.[164] The restructuring

---

[163]One commentator pointed out that 'the formation of a bank advisory group has no legal consequences and neither creates nor changes any legal or contractual relationship among the debtor, the bank advisory group or the banks at large', Mudge, *Perspective of Counsel*, at 66.

Although concluded at a later stage of the debt crisis, Brazil's agreement with its commercial bank creditors to clear interest arrears, reached in 1991 and described later in this study, provides an illustration of this perception regarding the non-binding nature of the acts of bank steering committees. Section 8.03 (Limitations on Liability of the Closing Agent and the Bank Advisory Committee for Brazil) of the Bond Exchange Agreement dated as of September 10, 1993, among Republica Federativa do Brasil and Citibank, NA, as Closing Agent and Others, provides:

> (b) *the Bank Advisory Committee for Brazil*. No member of the Bank Advisory Committee for Brazil, as such, shall have any duties or obligations whatsoever with respect to this Agreement or any other document or any matter related hereto, except as expressly provided in this Agreement.

[164]Deposit schemes on these lines were adopted, among other instances, in the Brazil restructuring packages from 1983 through 1988; and in the restructuring of Mexican private sector debt in 1983; Buchheit, Documentation Issues and

agreement might feature an on-lending, or re-lending, facility, whereby the deposited amounts could be the object of re-lending to a new borrower in the debtor country.

A deposit scheme as described along the general lines above amounts to a consolidation of debt, to the extent that debts owed under a plurality of loan instruments are reorganized under one single deposit account with the Central Bank. In addition, this consolidation of debt could feature a novation of debt – to the extent the Central Bank, or the Republic itself, substituted for the original borrowers as the obligor under the new contractual relationship. This substitution process is complex in time, since it only takes effect as the borrowers under the original loan agreements are discharged of their obligation by making local currency payments into the Central Bank account.

Refinancing In the main, the rationale for providing new money in the context of debt restructuring derived from creditors' concerns that an interruption in interest servicing would affect their income, as well as with the regulatory and accounting implications that such an event would entail. From a financial/ economic standpoint, providing new money was also a logical course of action given the then prevailing belief that the difficulties the debtor countries were facing amounted to a temporary liquidity crisis.[165]

The amount of new financing was calculated in accordance with an estimated external financing gap, once an appraisal of forthcoming contributions from other sources – multilateral and official creditors – had been made.[166] Commitments would be made on the basis of banks' exposure to the debtor as of an agreed base date; each bank would participate in a proportion

---

Alternative Techniques of Debt Restructuring, 1–28 LATIN AMERICAN SOVEREIGN DEBT MANAGEMENT, LEGAL AND REGULATORY ASPECTS (Ralph Reisner, Emilio J. Cardenas and Antonio Mendes editors, Washington DC, Inter-American Development Bank, 1990, 273p, at p. 20.

[165]For a complete description and discussion of the arrangement of refinancing packages, both in the initial phases of the crisis and later, see Stumpf, *Overview of Techniques*.

[166]Stumpf and Debevoise point out that 'the exercise also requires that assumptions be made concerning major economic variables such as OECD growth, interest rates and, frequently, key commodity prices'. According to the authors, the process is 'subtle, complicated and political', Stumpf, *Overview of Techniques*, at 55.

which reflected its share of the country's outstanding eligible debt.

In the initial period of the debt crisis, refinancing agreements took the form of a single syndicated eurodollar loan, which bore great resemblance to the syndicated loans which evidenced the original debts, with provisions regarding interest rate, covenants, conditions precedent, events of default and the like.[167] Although, from a factual point of view, the new money agreement clearly arose from the difficulties related to the execution of the original loan agreements, it was formally an autonomous legal instrument which created new rights and obligations for borrowers and creditors which were not necessarily the same parties to the underlying loan agreements.[168]

In the later phase of restructuring agreements, the trend toward securitization, discussed below, implied that refinancing began to take the form of the subscription, by creditor institutions, of new money bonds. Borrowers under the new money agreements would typically be the country's Central Bank, with the sovereign providing a guarantee; or the sovereign itself.

Adjustment   The third pillar of the debt strategy was the adoption of economic adjustment measures by the debtor country. In order to persuade debtors to adopt such measures, the provision of new funds was linked to the debtor countries reaching a stand-by[169] or extended arrangement[170] with the International Monetary

[167]Stumpf, *Overview of Techniques*, at 55.

[168]As Mudge points out, 'once executed, the new money credit agreement operates within its own contractual context and basically without reference to the debt outstanding under the universe of existing agreements between multiple debtors and bank creditors', Mudge, *Perspective of Counsel*, at 71.

[169]The body of norms governing the operations and transactions of the International Monetary Fund does not define stand-by or extended arrangements. Joseph Gold, former general counsel of the IMF, defines a stand-by arrangement as 'a decision of the Fund that gives a member the assurance that it will be able to make purchases of the Fund's general resources (. . .) during a specified period and up to a specified amount', Gold, Joseph, *Relations Between Bank's Loan Agreements and Fund Stand-by Arrangements*, 781–802 Gold, Joseph, LEGAL AND INSTITUTIONAL ASPECTS OF THE INTERNATIONAL MONETARY SYSTEM (1984) (hereinafter Gold, *Relations between Bank and Fund*) at 788.

The Fund's currency sales are the legal form used by the institution to channel financial assistance; the Fund avoids characterizing its arrangements with member countries as loan agreements. See Petersmann, FINANCIAL ASSISTANCE, at 25–26.

[170]Extended arrangements are usually subject to the Fund's policy governing stand-by arrangements. However, they differ from stand-by arrangements in two

Fund. Since the provision of balance of payment assistance by the IMF under both arrangements is accompanied by the establishment of 'performance criteria'[171] aimed at ensuring that the use of funds will be both effective in addressing the balance of payments problem, and temporary in nature, creditors could be confident that the necessary adjustment measures were being implemented by the debtor. It is in this context that the notion of 'conditionality' attached to IMF programs was tied into restructuring exercises.[172]

As regards documentation, the link to an IMF-sponsored program would be made through a provision in the agreement regarding some aspect of the borrower's relationship with the Fund. Thus, the parties to the restructuring agreement would agree that IMF Board approval of the stand-by or extended arrangement would constitute a condition precedent to a first disbursement under the commercial loan. Alternatively, disbursement was made conditional upon actual disbursement under the IMF arrangement;[173] subsequent disbursements could

regards at least: they are longer – usually three years; and they are designed to provide assistance associated with structural maladjustments. Gold, *Relations between Bank and Fund* at 787 and 789.

[171]'Obvious examples of performance criteria are quantitative limits of a financial or economic character that are not to be exceeded, such as the volume of credit expansion by the central bank, or quantitative targets of a financial or economic character that are to be reached, such as the reduction in international payment arrears', Gold, *Relations between Bank and Fund* at 789.

[172]According to Gold, 'that word connotes the standards that a member's economic and financial program must meet to satisfy the requirements of the particular policy involving conditionality to which the member wishes to resort', Gold, *Relations between Bank and Fund* at 783. Article V, section 3(b) of the IMF's Articles of Agreement provide the general authority for the imposition of conditionality.

For a critical analysis of IMF-sponsored programs under stand-by arrangements, see Knieper, Rolf, *The Conditioning of National Policy-Making by International Law: The Standby Arrangements of the International Monetary Fund*, 41–64 INTERNATIONAL JOURNAL OF THE SOCIOLOGY OF LAW no. 11 (1983).

[173]Stumpf, *Overview of Techniques*, at 59–60. See also Gold, Joseph, ORDER IN INTERNATIONAL FINANCE, THE PROMOTION OF STAND-BY ARRANGEMENTS AND THE DRAFTING OF PRIVATE LOAN AGREEMENTS IMF Brochure no. 39. Washington DC, IMF, 1982; Higgins, *Sovereign Lending and IMF Conditionality*, IFLR May 1984; Edwards, Richard W., *Is an IMF Stand-by Arrangement a 'Seal of Approval' on which other Creditors can Rely?* 573–597 NEW YORK UNIVERSITY JOURNAL OF INTERNATIONAL LAW AND POLITICS vol. 17 (1985).

Sir Joseph Gold warns that 'if provisions are not drafted with expert knowledge of the law and practice of the Fund, the assurance may be illusory or ambiguous', Gold, *Relations between Bank and Fund*, at 782. In the article, the former General Counsel of the Fund discusses the types of provisions commonly used, as well as their effectiveness and implications.

be made conditional upon further drawings under the IMF facilities. Another variation had the parties establish that the member State's ceasing to be in regular standing under the Fund's facility would constitute an event of default under the loan agreement.[174]

With the adoption of the practice of multi-year reschedulings the strict linkage between disbursements under the commercial new money loan to disbursements under an IMF stand-by arrangement presented practical difficulties, in that the period covered under the restructuring agreement would often go beyond the tenor of the relevant Fund facility. Accordingly, the provision requiring that the member be subject to IMF surveillance under the consultation procedures provided for under Article IV of the Fund's Articles of Agreement gradually replaced the more stringent disbursement clauses in restructuring packages.[175]

The strategy revised: the Brady restructurings

While the strategy initially devised to cope with the developing country debt crisis of the 1980s did prevent the major crisis in the international financial system that would have come about as a result of generalized default, the basic assumptions on which it lay proved incorrect. Temporary financial relief to debtors coupled with internal adjustment did not allow for lasting economic recovery and restored capacity to meet external debt obligations. Instead, restructuring exercises became a recurrent need.[176]

[174]The use of event of default clauses to effect the linkage with an IMF program is clearly much less effective than making disbursement under the loan agreement conditional upon the country's maintaining such a program, given the essential importance of disbursement for the borrower and creditors' notorious reluctance in invoking the event of default clauses in the context of developing countries external debt difficultites.

Reference to the borrower's maintaining a Fund facility would also be included as a covenant in the new money agreement – that is, a commitment undertaken by the relevant borrower in the form a contractually sanctioned obligation to maintain such Fund facility. However, the purpose of the provision here would be more to assure contribution from official sources in filling the country's external financing gap than ensuring the adoption of adjustment measures. See Stumpf, *Overview of Techniques*, at 61.

[175]See commentary in 25 ILM 477 (1986) on this evolution.

[176]As pointed out by one commentator in the early years of the debt crisis:

[many] reschedulings in recent years have required subsequent rescheduling, and creditor banks have been known to acknowledge, in the course of

The cycle of renewed restructuring agreements represented great inconveniences for borrowers and lenders alike. To be sure, rescheduling of the stock of the debt was an essential relief of the financial obligations hanging over a debtor. However, the burden of interest payment obligations alone proved to be excessive to most; this resulted, in several instances, in the mounting of interest arrears which also had to be renegotiated in the context of restructuring agreements.[177]

From the standpoint of lenders, recurrent restructuring exercises meant renewed new money calls. The making of new money commitments to debtors which were notoriously facing grave financial difficulties constituted in itself a great inconvenience.[178] The problem worsened because of the negative regulatory and accounting implications that such new money commitments might entail for some of the lenders involved. Under the regulations of some industrial countries, new money commitments to financially troubled borrowers might require automatic provisioning. This would be particularly worrisome for those banks acting under a regulatory environment which did not allow specific loan loss reserves to be included in the definition of capital; for them, LDC reserves meant immobilized

negotiations, that before the ink is dry on one rescheduling agreement, a new agreement will be required.

Wickersham, Warren G., *Problems of Documentation in Rescheduling of Sovereign Bank Debt*, 117–123 DEFAULT AND RESCHEDULING. CORPORATE AND SOVEREIGN BORROWERS IN DIFFICULTY (David Suratgar editor), London, Euromoney, 1984, 163p., at 118.

[177]Buchheit points out that:

> [In some countries] the interest component of the debt may itself prove an insupportable burden in light of unexpected declines in the price of important exports. (. . .) Moreover, requiring interest payments to remain current may drain an alarming amount of the country's foreign currency earnings, leaving little to finance the economic recovery necessary to restore debt service capability.

Buchheit, Lee C., *Documentation Issues and Alternative Techniques of Debt Restructuring*, 1–28 LATIN AMERICAN SOVEREIGN DEBT MANAGEMENT. LEGAL AND REGULATORY ASPECTS (Ralph Reisner, Emilio J. Cardenas and Antonio Mendes editors), Washington DC, Inter-American Development Bank, 1990, 273p. (Buchheit, *Alternative Debt Restructuring*), at 8.

[178]See, in general, Davis, Richard J., *Coping with 'Fatigue' in the Debt-Restructuring Process*, 147–153 CURRENT LEGAL ISSUES AFFECTING CENTRAL BANKS, in particular at p. 148.

resources and reduced leverage.[179] This factor made new money commitments more costly for those banks.

A parallel factor explained banks' increased desire – and ability – to avoid agreements which entailed new money commitments. Since the beginning of the debt crisis, major creditor banks had been gradually strengthening their capital base. Also, as from 1987 there came about a clear trend towards setting aside specific reserves for losses in claims against developing country debtors. Both factors increased creditor banks' ability to enter agreements entailing write-offs of their claims, as opposed to mere deferment of principal installments. They also increased the desire among banks to rid themselves of LDC loans altogether.[180]

The increased capital base, coupled with adequate reserves, set the stage for the adoption of renegotiation procedures which comprised debt-reduction instruments. Such procedures came about with the adoption of the 'menu-approach' to the restructuring of sovereign debt, whereunder creditors were offered a set of instruments in exchange for their outstanding claims.

The new strategy gained official endorsement with the March 1989 pronouncement of US Secretary of the Treasury, in which he expressly stated that:

> [commercial] banks need to work with debtor nations to provide a broader range of alternatives for financial support, including greater efforts to achieve both debt and debt service reduction and to provide new lending. The approach to this problem must be realistic. The path toward greater creditworthiness and a return to the markets for many debtor countries must include debt reduction.[181]

---

[179]For a comparative survey of the treatment of loss reserves for claims against developing country debtors, see Hay, REGULATION OF BANKS.

[180]This led to the development, beginning in 1986–1987, of an active secondary market among banks for the trading of their claims against developing country borrowers.

[181]Statement of Nicholas F. Brady, 69–76 THIRD WORLD DEBT: THE NEXT PHASE (Edward R. Fried and Philip H. Trezise editors), Washington DC, The Brookings Institution, 1989, 118p. (*Report of a Conference held in Washington DC, on March 10, 1989.*)

The so-called 'Brady Plan' replaced the previous official US strategy, as announced by Brady's predecessor, Secretary James Baker, of 'adjustment with growth' – but without debt reduction. See Statement of the Honorable James A. Baker, III, Secretary of the Treasury of the United States before the Joint Annual Meeting of the International Monetary Fund and the World Bank, October 8, 1985, Seoul, Korea, Treasury News Releases.

Under the 'menu' approach to the restructuring of developing country external indebtedness, along the lines of the so-called Brady Plan, outstanding indebtedness would be exchanged for bonds with longer maturities[182] issued either by the country's Central Bank, or by the sovereign itself. The expression 'menu' is related to the fact that creditors were offered a set of options under the agreement, each relating to a new instrument having differing characteristics including, without limitation, maturity, grace period, interest rate structure and degree of collateralization, if any. Such variety of instruments is theoretically aimed at compatibilizing debtors' need for debt or debt service reduction with cash flow relief, on the one hand, with differing factors – including regulatory, tax and accounting considerations – which determined creditors' ability to participate in the debt restructuring exercise on the other hand.

The reduction element contained in the agreement would regard the stock of the debt, as well as interest payments. Reduction of the stock of outstanding indebtedness is achieved through the exchange of eligible debt, at a discount, for bonds with a discounted face value – 'discount bonds' – and market interest rates. Debt service reduction, in turn, would stem from the exchange of eligible debt, at par, for an instrument – a par bond – with fixed rate of interest at levels below market for at least part of the life of the instrument.

In some instances, agreements also featured voluntary new money financing through the inclusion in the 'menu' of a new money option, whereby creditors exchange eligible credits for a debt conversion bond with a corresponding obligation to subscribe new money bonds. Other variations of Brady agreements featured debt buybacks with cash, at a steep discount, or the exchange of debt for collateralized short-term notes, also at a discount which would otherwise not be acceptable to creditors were the exchange not for a short-term instrument.

In order to enhance the attractiveness of the package, and out of concern with the regulatory treatment of claims against developing country borrowers, the par and discount bonds were typically collateralized with respect to principal, as well as with respect to a given number of months of interest payments. Principal collateral would take the form of the pledge of US Treasury

---

[182]Usually thirty years.

zero coupon bonds of the same tenor as the collateralized par and discount bonds, or equivalent securities in other currencies. Interest collateral, in turn, would take the form of a deposit in a special account with a collateral agent of an amount sufficient to secure interest payments in the agreed number of months.

Since the par and discount bonds were usually 'bullet', with the principal being repaid in one single installment at final maturity, the acquisition of principal collateral upon the initial issuance of the bonds meant the debtor country could use the proceeds from the redemption of the Treasury bonds pledged as collateral to redeem its own indebtedness. Additional features might be included so as to enhance the attractiveness of the instruments, such as eligibility for conversion in debt–equity programs.

The acquisition of the collateral for the guaranteed instruments required, on the part of the restructuring country, disbursement of substantial amounts of foreign exchange. The country would typically draw for that purpose from its own international reserves and from whatever new money was forthcoming as a result of subscription, by creditors, of the new money option, if any; as well as from official sources.

Official support for debt restructuring packages under the Brady Plan was given in the form of financing from the international financial institutions for the purchase of the collateral. Hence, the International Monetary Fund, the International Bank for Reconstruction and Development, as well as the Inter-American Development Bank, have devised, since the announcement of the Brady Plan, debt and debt-service reduction programs, whereby a portion of each institution's resource flows for the country in question under the respective financing programs could be set aside for the purchase of collateral.[183]

As regards documentation, the initial term sheet for the deal typically unfolded into implementing agreements, including

[183]The Executive Board of the IMF adopted, on May 23, 1989, guidelines for the use of the Fund's resources in debt and debt service reduction transactions; see Dooley, Michael P., and Watson, C. Maxwell, *Reinvigorating the Debt Strategy*, 8–11 FINANCE & DEVELOPMENT, September 1989, at 8. The World Bank's Executive Directors approved similar guidelines on May 31, 1989; see Husain, Ishrat, *Recent Experience with the Debt Strategy*, 12–16 FINANCE & DEVELOPMENT, September 1989, at 15; and Shihata, Ibrahim, THE WORLD BANK IN A CHANGING WORLD. SELECTED ESSAYS, Dordrecht, Martinus Nijhoff, 1991, 490p., at 27. The Inter-American Development Bank approved a similar program through Resolution AG-10/90, dated October 15, 1990.

bond exchange agreements for the various options, which replaced the subscription agreement under a fresh bond transaction; a fiscal agency agreement;[184] as well as bond indentures.[185] In the case of a new money option, the documentation also includes a new money bond subscription agreement.

In terms of contract adaptation, the restructuring agreements along the lines of the Brady Plan amount to a novation of the outstanding agreements. The novation occurs, on the one hand, to the extent that the terms of the debt are modified – including maturity, interest rate and repayment schedule. This modification is qualified by the fact that the original indebtedness, which is in most cases unsecured, is exchanged for a basket of options which include collateralized instruments. In addition, the novation also exists in respect to the exchange of debtors: the new instruments under the restructuring agreement were usually issued by the central government of the restructuring country, and occasionally by the Central Bank, which replace the original obligor under the creditor–debtor relationship.[186]

---

[184]Although uncommon, debt restructuring documentation has also included a trust deed, as in the 1990 Nigerian debt restructuring agreement.

[185]Which may be defined as 'a written agreement under which bonds and debentures are issued, setting forth form of bond, maturity date, amount of issue, description of pledged assets, interest rate, and other terms', BLACK'S LAW DICTIONARY, abridged 6th edition, 1991.

[186]Subject, of course, to the extent that the issuer was already the obligor under the restructured indebtedness. Such novation also implies, on the internal front, that arrangements are made between the issuer of the new instruments and the original obligors for the refinancing of the restructured indebtedness. These arrangements are not without difficulties, legal and political alike.

Part II:

ADAPTATION CLAUSES

The experience of the developing country debt crisis of the 1980s underlined the rigidity of the legal instruments used to channel development financing in the 1970s and early 1980s in relation to external changes in circumstances affecting borrowers' ability to meet payment obligations.[187]

Any attempt to ascertain whether the crisis would have been avoided or mitigated had original loan documentation provided for relief against the adverse changes that borrowers faced under the circumstances which prompted the crisis would probably amount to a speculative effort. It is nevertheless submitted that contractual flexibility would have smoothed the impact of the external shocks, and might have prevented the overall contract disruption which the crisis provoked. Adaptation provided for in the relevant, original governing instruments would have obviated dealing with changed circumstances in an *ad hoc* manner, in the context of hazardous, time-consuming restructuring exercises which often interrupted resource flows to the developing country in question for long periods of time, and which brought to creditors' balance sheets too great an element of uncertainty.

While lack of contractual flexibility with respect to borrowers' obligations under adverse circumstances was a marked feature of loan agreements outstanding at the time of the debt crisis of

---

[187]While the inconvenience that such rigidity represented was sufficiently analyzed in the economic literature, it has hardly been discussed by legal scholars. For a general discussion, see Silard, Stephen, *International Law and the Conditions for Order in International Finance: Lessons of the Debt Crisis*, 963–976 THE INTERNATIONAL LAWYER vol. 23, winter 1989, especially at 975.

the 1980s, documentation evidencing resumed private debt capital flows to developing countries, on the other hand, does not depart from such pattern of contractual rigidity as regards adaptation to adverse changes in circumstances.

Contractual flexibility designed to cushion the adverse effects of external shocks and to preserve contractual relationships under financing transactions is theoretically attainable through the inclusion of adaptation mechanisms in the relevant documentation. The discussion of adaptation mechanisms which a developing country borrower and its creditors under a transnational financing transaction can conceivably agree to write into their contract will be undertaken in the present part of this study. The starting point of the discussion will be adaptation provisions included in documentation arising out of restructuring agreements in connection with the debt crisis.[188] In addition to such provisions, other types of adaptation mechanisms have been discussed in the economic literature;[189] most of them can be assimilated, as to their effects, to one or another of the modalities of provisions examined below.

It should be recalled that protection against adverse changes in circumstances should be viewed in the overall framework of a particular debtor's liability management strategy, which includes the resort to market-based, derivative instruments. As submitted in Chap. 2 of this study, however, contractually foreseen adaptation should ideally be resorted to as a complement to market-based instruments, whenever these are available; and

[188]This author was a member of the government team that negotiated Brazil's 1993 debt restructuring agreement with a bank steering committee chaired by Citibank, NA, while working with the legal department of Brazil's Ministry of Finance. He later joined a São Paulo law firm active in the issue of eurobonds by Brazilian corporate borrowers. The documentation on which the following discussion is based was obtained in connection with such experience.

In addition to loan agreements evidencing restructured indebtedness, the documentation reviewed includes term sheets for various sovereign debt restructuring agreements concluded throughout the 1980s and early 1990s; implementing agreements in the case of the Brady restructuring packages, including bond exchange agreements, fiscal agency agreements and bond indentures; and documentation relating to fresh bond issues by Brazilian borrowers, including subscription and agency agreements and trust deeds.

[189]See, in particular, the study prepared by the Washington-based Institute for International Economics, Bergstein, C. Fred, Cline, William R., and Williamson, John, BANK LENDING TO DEVELOPING COUNTRIES: THE POLICY ALTERNATIVES, Washington DC, Institute for International Economics, April 1985, 210p. (Bergsten, BANK LENDING), at 42–58.

as the main form of protection, in those cases where the market does not provide alternatives.

The question regarding typology of adaptation clauses was discussed in Part 1 of this study. According to the definitions adopted, the discussion of adaptation clauses will follow a general distinction between provisions related to procedure, i.e. renegotiation clauses, and provisions related to substance – adaptation clauses *stricto sensu*. The analysis of different types of adaptation provisions will be preceded by an introductory discussion to the topic and followed by a discussion of the likelihood that adaptation clauses be adopted in development financing in a generalized manner.

Chapter Four

GENERAL ASPECTS OF ADAPTATION

The two types of development financing transactions which provide the background for the discussion of adaptation clauses undertaken in this study are syndicated bank credits and bond issues, both of which have been reviewed earlier. The features of bond issues that render its documentation less compatible with adaptation provisions than loan agreements will be briefly discussed in the following. The question regarding the regulatory constraints that could constitute an obstacle to the generalized inclusion of adaptation provisions in instruments governing development financing transactions will follow.

From the outset, it should be noted that in addition to adaptation mechanisms, discussed in chaps 5, 6 and 7 of this study, the contractual framework for the protection of borrowers against adverse changes in circumstances is completed by a set of contractual provisions which, while not entailing modification of the contract itself, allow borrowers flexibility regarding liability management.[190] Thus, bond documentation under the various Brady Plans contains, to varying degrees, provisions which enable the issuer to take advantage of favorable market circumstances and undertake transactions targeted at the optimization of its debt profile.

Hence, an issuer under a bond subscription or exchange agreement may attempt to capture a discount, if any, in the secondary market for its own indebtedness, as well as benefit from a favorable balance of payments position, in the case of a sovereign borrower, by structuring transactions under which it repurchases the bonds in question, redeems them earlier than the scheduled

---

[190]The use of derivatives, discussed in Chap. 1 of this study, should be added to such contractual mechanisms in completing the framework of risk-hedging.

maturity, or indirectly refinances them under a debt-for-debt exchange. Similar provisions may be agreed in the context of a bond issue by a private sector borrower. The actual range of permissible transactions will of course depend on the terms of the relevant agreements. The survey of such clauses escapes the scope of this study, and will not be undertaken.

Adaptation of bonds v. adaptation of loans

Due to aspects related to documentation, as a general matter loan agreements concluded between a developing country borrower and a given bank creditor, or a group of banks organized under a syndicate, constitute a more appropriate environment for experimenting with adaptation provisions than does documentation related to a bond issue. Parties to a loan agreement can conceivably shape it to meet their needs and interests, while bond documentation is considerably less elastic, as briefly discussed in Part II.

The fact that bond issues are less amenable to the inclusion of adaptation mechanisms than bank credits is further explained by the nature of the creditors under the respective transactions. Commercial banks have the expertise and sophistication required to evaluate and build features into a particular financing transaction which depart from standard practice. By contrast, the dispersion in ownership of bonds, itself a consequence of their marked negotiability – particularly in the case of bearer bonds, requires a corresponding standardization in the relevant documentation. As mentioned earlier, the fact that investments in securities are often managed on behalf of final bondholders by highly sophisticated professional portfolio managers does not alter this scenario, since the search for relatively standard terms is foremost in marketing the instruments. In addition, while a borrower and its creditors under a bank loan will typically negotiate the terms of their transaction directly, such direct interaction does not exist in the case of a bond issue, where the terms and conditions of the instruments are negotiated between the issuer and the managers of the issue, and are binding upon the ultimate bondholders.

Interestingly enough, bond documentation arising out of Brady restructuring agreements in connection with the debt crisis, discussed above, features the adoption of mechanisms providing for some form of contractual flexibility; such documentation will indeed be the starting point for the following discussion of adaptation provisions.

Although such clauses do indicate a departure from the pattern of rigidity regarding borrowers' obligations that has characterized development financing transactions to date, it remains true that sovereign bond issues in connection with restructuring agreements present some peculiarities which turn them into precedents of relative value only. Indeed, contractual arrangements implementing restructuring agreements were tailored to meet the specific needs of each restructuring situation. Hence, interest capitalization provisions – one type of adaptation clause discussed below – were agreed to in some instances as a result of the need to provide the restructuring country with cash flow relief in the initial years of the agreement. Value recovery mechanisms, in turn, were designed to make up for debt or debt service reduction, as discussed below.

The fact that bonds issued in connection with debt restructuring agreements were not initially subscribed by a wide universe of investors, but instead placed in the hands of a given universe of creditor banks whose claims were being exchanged for the bonds in question, is particularly relevant for the present discussion. Although the 'Brady' bonds gained a life of their own upon issuance, the negotiation of their terms took place between the renegotiating country and a creditor bank committee – not between the debtor and an agent, or group of agent banks, who would subsequently place the instruments with investors at large, as under an ordinary bond issue. As a consequence, the creditors involved disposed of much larger leeway to negotiate unprecedented adaptation provisions than would managers of a regular bond issue. This reservation should hold even though such bonds were subsequently transferable in the market-place.

While the peculiarities of bond issues in connection with debt restructuring agreements should be borne in mind, the pace at which securities markets evolve would seem to suggest that obstacles to the generalization of what today may be seen as exotic adaptation mechanisms in the context of a market-based bond issue may no longer subsist in a near future. Other considerations aside, the fact that such mechanisms were included in the documentation related to debt restructuring-related bond issues demonstrates that, from the standpoint of legal technique, such mechanisms are not incompatible with documentation related to bond issues. This assertion seems to be corroborated by the fact that adaptation mechanisms have also been included, to some extent, in issues by industrialized country borrowers.[191]

Regulatory constraints to adaptation

The evolution of the debt crisis of the 1980s demonstrates that the decisions taken by commercial banks were, to a considerable extent, determined by incentives and constraints provided by the tax, accounting and regulatory environment under which they operate. Accordingly, the feasibility of adaptation clauses in documentation related to LDC lending is largely dependent on whether creditors, and in particular bank creditors, would derive any benefits – or incur any losses – in agreeing to them.

While definitive answers as to the regulatory, tax and accounting implications of individual mechanism would require a thorough analysis of relevant rules under each domestic legal system, it would seem, as a general proposition, that the clauses discussed in the following would not be hindered by any fundamental tax, accounting or regulatory constraints if agreed to by negotiation in connection with voluntary lending.

Surveys of the current status of relevant regulations across the major industrialized countries seem to indicate that where constraints or unfavorable treatment of specific mechanisms exist, it is mostly in connection with actual or perceived problems regarding borrowers' ability to meet payment obligations.[192] The rationale for the adverse treatment, if any, is tied to the perception of danger regarding the collectibility of the asset.[193] This rationale

[191]See Privolos, Theophilos, *Experience with Commodity-Linked Issues*, 11–38 COMMODITY RISK MANAGEMENT AND FINANCE (Theophilos Privolos and Ronald C. Duncan editors), Washington DC, Oxford University Press, 1991 (hereinafter Privolos, *Commodity-Linked Issues*), at 11.

[192]See Hay, REGULATION OF BANKS. This study builds upon the comprehensive previous study of Hay, Jonathan, and Bouchet, Michel H., THE TAX, ACCOUNTING AND REGULATORY TREATMENT OF SOVEREIGN DEBT, Washington DC, World Bank Cofinancing and Financial Advisory Services Department, September 1989, 99p. See also the analysis of individual adaptation mechanisms undertaken in Bergstein, BANK LENDING, at 95–196.

[193]That is generally true, for instance, of the treatment of non-accrual loans, that is, loans in relation to which interest income ceases to be accrued. In the UK, 'most banks state that interest on advances, up until the normal banking relationship with the customer has ceased, is credited to the profit and loss account and

would no longer hold, it is submitted, if absence of interest payments, for instance, in connection with an interest capitalization clause, were the result of agreement between the parties.[194]

A *renegotiation clause* would not in itself entail any negative tax, accounting or regulatory treatment for banks, for all it represents is a duty to rediscuss the terms of the contract in light of the changed circumstances. Regulatory incentives and constraints to banks would clearly vary *ex post* according to whether the process

provision is made where appropriate'; Hay, REGULATION OF BANKS, at 35. In Canada, 'non-accrual loans are loans on which interest is not being accrued due to the existence of reasonable doubt as to the ultimate collectibility of principal or interest', Hay, REGULATION OF BANKS, at 81. In the US:

> the decision to stop accruing interest income on loans is based on management's evaluation as to the collectibility of the interest and principal. (. . .) For uniformity in financial reporting [the Officer of the Comptroller of the Currency] has adopted a policy for nonaccrual of interest on delinquent loans. Banks may not accrue interest on any loan when principal or interest are in default for 90 days or more unless the loan is well secured and in the process of collection.

Hay, REGULATION OF BANKS, at 109. In France, '(. . .) once a loan has been classified as "doubtful" (. . .) interest thereon would normally be provided for; the decision to place a loan in doubtful status is a management decision and no fixed rules apply', Hay, REGULATION OF BANKS, at 170.

[194]Although the question has, at the time of writing, apparently not been directly elucidated by regulators, this understanding is endorsed by commentators. According to Hurlock:

> [the regulators] would not be bound to require additional reserves or disclosure under the [Allocated Transfer Risk Reserves] and SEC regulations if they viewed capping arrangements as contractual agreements fixing the interest due at any payment date to the stated cap rate and treated the amounts payable with respect to any interest as amounts due under a separate legal obligation.

Hurlock, James B., *Legal Implications of Interest Rate Caps on Loans to Sovereign Borrowers*, 543–552 NEW YORK JOURNAL OF INTERNATIONAL LAW AND POLITICS vol. 17 (1985) (hereinafter Hurlock, *Interest Rate Caps*), at 550–551.

> According to a 1985 study by the Institute for International Economics: [in general], when deferral [of interest] arises as the consequence of provisions in the original loan agreement, deferred interest is likely to be accruable into current income. The original terms of the loan are being met and the loan presumably has incorporated a risk premium that compensates the lender; the instrument is market based.

Bergstein, BANK LENDING ALTERNATIVES at 26; see also p. 139 in the same sense.

A 1987 study by the same Institute concluded that: '(. . .) if the bank in question had agreed contractually to a capitalization of interest, the loan might not have to be treated as delinquent by regulators,' Cline, MOBILIZING BANK LENDING, at 23.

The tax treatment of interest capitalization, however, is more of an open question.

leads to interest capping, contingency financing, interest capitalization or any other specific adaptation mechanism.

Interest capping in the strict sense, on the other hand, would in all likelihood receive an adverse treatment, since placing a cap on interest and forgiving whatever portion is above that cap amounts to taking an actual loss, which would have to be recognized. This is why such clauses do not fit into a context of voluntary lending, as discussed below.

As a general matter, *contingency financing* provisions would not carry negative treatment if the borrower to which the new financing is committed is perceived as creditworthy. In the context of refinancing under restructuring agreements entered in the later phases of the debt crisis, new money tended to be avoided because it might require automatic provisioning under some lender countries' regulations. The rationale for this requirement was related to the perception that the underlying loans were impaired. Should contingency financing be agreed contractually, in connection with 'fresh' loan agreements concluded under voluntary lending, and designed essentially to provide some breathing room to fundamentally sound borrowers, there would submittedly be no reason to treat the new commitments in an unfavorable manner. On the other hand, the feasibility of contingency financing would also need to be examined in light of regulations related to risk concentration and lending limits.

Again, the practicability of each specific adaptation mechanism would of course have to be evaluated in regard to each particular transaction, and to each domestic regulatory system involved, a task which goes beyond the scope of the present study.

Chapter Five

RENEGOTIATION CLAUSES

Renegotiation clauses require parties to a contract to seek to modify the terms of their agreement should certain circumstances, beyond the control of either party, occur in a fashion which significantly alters the balance of the contract.[195]

Renegotiation clauses do not impose upon either party the duty to reach substantive agreement to modify the terms of the contract. The duty imposed by renegotiation clauses does not refer to results but to procedure: rather than providing for automatic adjustment of the agreement, renegotiation clauses require the parties to consult with the aim of reaching a modification of the terms of the contract.

Certain requirements are usually singled out as constituting essential elements of a renegotiation clause. Hence, the circum-

---

[195]As used in the following discussion, the notion of renegotiation clauses is interchangeable with that of hardship clauses, sometimes discussed in the literature as a type of renegotiation clause:

> hardship clauses are a specific type of renegotiation clause, since they should only apply in exceptional situations, which the parties do not expect or at least do not want to occur. Beyond that aspect, hardship clauses present all the usual characteristics of renegotiation clauses with regard to procedure and sanctions.

Peter, ARBITRATION AND RENEGOTIATION, at 34; also, Peter, *Adaptation and Renegotiation*, at 157. On hardship in general, see also the articles by van Ommeslaghe, and Ullmann, cited above.

The notion will be used in the meaning given by Gold:

> A hardship clause can be described as a term of a contract under which the contract can be reviewed if a change in circumstances occurs that fundamentally modifies the initial balance between the obligations of the parties, so that performance, though not impossible, becomes unusually onerous for one party.

Gold, FLUCTUATING EXCHANGE RATES, at 226.

stances which have arisen must be beyond the control of either party.[196] They must alter the contractual balance in a substantive manner, so as to have made it excessively burdensome for one of the parties to perform its obligations. In addition, the events must be uncontemplated or unforeseeable.[197]

It remains true, however, that renegotiation clauses are what the parties to the agreement decide to make them. This is particularly true with regard to the element of unforeseeability, which may not be required.[198]

The main perceived advantage of a renegotiation clause regards the preservation of the contractual relationship under a setting which is essentially different from the original one.[199] Seen in light of the debt crisis of the 1980s, the inclusion of renegotiation clauses might not seem to alter substantially the framework for the adaptation of loan agreements, since this was the *de facto* course of action in the context of the debt crisis, as described above. However, while in the absence of a renegotiation provision parties are free to renegotiate the terms of the contract, a renegotiation clause *compels* them to do so should the specified events occur.[200]

---

[196]According to Schmithoff, *Hardship Clauses*, at 418–419 'self-induced hardship is irrelevant'. See also Horn, *Standard Clauses on Contract Adaptation*, at 132–135; Oppetit, *L'adaptation des contrats*, at 800–804; Boughaba, *Clauses d'adaptation*, at 277–282.

[197]These requirements turn the notion of renegotiation into something similar to that of frustration under the requirements of domestic legal systems. Boughaba, *Clauses d'adaptation*, at 269.

[198]'Hardship clauses, by contrast, can apply, if the parties wish, to supervening events that were foreseen as possible when the contract was made (. . .)', Gold, FLUCTUATING EXCHANGE RATES, at 227. Oppetit suggests that the notion of *exteriority* is more suitable; Oppetit, *L'Adaptation des contrats*, at 801.

[199]'The object of a hardship clause is by way of renegotiation to convert the contractual relationship from a static into an evolutionary one', Schmithoff, *Hardship Clauses*, at 419. Peter, ARBITRATION AND RENEGOTIATION, at 32, is of the opinion that:

Renegotiation provisions, while indeed showing a willingness of the parties to change, can, at the same time, also represent a means of stabilizing the contract, since their purpose is to regulate and consequently delineate contract change.

[200]Gold comments on the mandatory nature of renegotiation under a hardship clause:

Contracting parties are free to renegotiate their contract at any time after entering into it. An advantage of a hardship clause is that it compels the parties to consider the modification of their contract if the existence of

It remains true the sanction for non-fulfillment of the obligation to negotiate in good faith may at times be awkward to formulate in the agreement itself, and difficult to enforce after the fact.[201] Provisions in the agreement may contemplate the precise procedure to be followed, and the intervention of a third party failing agreement of the parties, in which case the renegotiation clause would probably gain in effectiveness.[202] Should on the other hand the clause fail to provide for the procedure and sanctions of the failure to agree, the injured party would have to resort to arbitration or litigation. The extent to which an arbitral tribunal or a court could substitute for the parties and alter the terms of the contract is itself not without difficulties.[203]

On the face of it, renegotiation clauses could be preferable to lenders over provisions which entail automatic adaptation because of the interest on the part of lenders to monitor closely the behavior and management of borrowers. Such control is relinquished once automatic adaptation is agreed to.[204]

In reality, however, the uncertainty as to the results of the renegotiation process that such clauses imply makes renego-

---

hardship is not disputed. There is no such compulsion in absence of a hardship clause.

Gold, FLUCTUATING EXCHANGE RATES, at 229.

[201]Oppetit suggests the obligation parties undertake under a renegotiation clause go a little beyond simply negotiating in good faith; indeed they would be under the duty to accept a reasonable proposal:

While stopping short of concluding in favor of the existence of a stringent duty to reach a modification, one can nevertheless consider that the requirements of good faith, as well as the intent of the parties, expressed by the very existence of a hardship clause, create upon the parties the duty to make a reasonable proposal, and to accept such a proposal, respectively, lest either party incur liability for breach of contract.

Oppetit, L'Adaptation des contrats, at 807; translation supplied.

[202]'A hardship clause without sanctions is hardly worth the paper on which it is written', Schmithoff, Hardship Clauses, at 420.

[203]See, Peter, Wolfgang, ARBITRATION AND RENEGOTIATION OF INTERNATIONAL INVESTMENT AGREEMENTS. A STUDY WITH PARTICULAR REFERENCE TO MEANS OF CONFLICT AVOIDANCE UNDER NATURAL RESOURCES INVESTMENT AGREEMENTS, 2nd edition, 1995. According to the author, most renegotiation clauses do not provide for the procedure to be followed during the renegotiation, or for the sanction attached to failure to agree.

[204]It is in this regard that one speaks of the benefits of the 'short leash'. Buchheit, Lee C., Documentation Issues and Alternative Techniques of Debt Restructuring, 1–28 LATIN AMERICAN SOVEREIGN DEBT MANAGEMENT. LEGAL AND REGULATORY ASPECTS (Ralph Reisner, Emilio J. Cardenas and Antonio Mendes editors), Washington DC, Inter-American Development Bank, 1990, 273 p., at 11–12.

tiation clauses ill-fitted in the eyes of lenders. Automatic adaptation, discussed below, is arguably acceptable to creditors because the modification process is – supposedly – swift, and the outcome of the process occurs within a predictable range of events. Renegotiation, by contrast, usually entails a complex time- and resource-consuming process which it would arguably be in the interest of both parties to avoid by providing in the contract for automatic adaptation.[205] The nature of the transaction and the relative positions of parties may help explain why a renegotiation process may be more acceptable to an investor under agreements to prospect oil in a developing country, for instance, than to lenders under an international financing transaction.[206]

Albeit in the field of debt restructuring with official creditors, bilateral negotiations involving Brazil under its Paris Club Agreed Minute of February 26, 1992 illustrate the controversy over the advantages of a renegotiation clause in international financing transactions. The controversy arose as a result of the passing of legislation in Brazil – Senate Resolution 82, of 1990 – requiring authorities to include in any external financing agreement to which the Republic or its instrumentalities are a party provisions which protect the relevant obligor from changes in circumstances.[207]

In the course of bilateral negotiations under the auspices of

[205]It should be noted, however, that parties can conceivably shape the renegotiation provision so as to establish a time limit for the process.

[206]An official from one major commercial bank with headquarters in New York noted that he would not be in a position to propose to the credit committee of his institution a loan which contemplated from the outset the possibility that its repayment terms be subsequently modified due to distress suffered by the borrower. Interviews in New York, January 24, 1993.

[207]Article 52 of the 1988 Brazilian Federal Constitution conferred upon the Brazilian Senate exclusive competence to authorize any external financing transactions involving the Central Government, as well as to issue directives applicable to such transactions. Under the latter authority, the Brazilian Senate issued Resolution 82, dated December 18, 1990, which set the requirement for a renegotiation clause. The relevant provision of Resolution 82 reads:

Article 4 – Agreements relating to external financing transactions to which the Central Government (a União) or its instrumentalities (*autarquias*) are a party
IV – shall contain a clause providing for the possibility of modifying the contract, whenever this is necessary to restore the contractual balance, which may have been disrupted as a result of material supervening changes in the circumstances prevailing at the time the agreement was concluded, and not caused by either party to the contract. (translation supplied).

the Paris Club, negotiators for the Brazilian government insisted with each team of representatives of foreign official creditors that a renegotiation clause be written into the relevant agreement. Creditors' reactions varied widely. While some creditor countries, or agencies thereof, offered no resistance to the inclusion of a clause to that effect, others objected strongly. It was argued, among other things, that renegotiation was of the very essence of the Paris Club conversations, and therefore no express provision was necessary.

Along with the requirement for an express renegotiation clause, Senate Resolution 82 also required that agreements contain an arbitration provision, which also proved an obstacle to the successful course of the bilateral negotiations. In addition, Senate Resolution 7, of April 1992, which specifically authorized the execution of bilateral agreements under the Paris Club Agreed Minute, imposed a cap to the spread over interest rate that the Brazilian Executive Power was authorized to accept under the implementing agreements. All three requirements caused difficulties for the bilateral negotiations.

To overcome such difficulties, the Brazilian Executive formally required the Senate to exempt specifically from such requirements the Paris Club bilateral restructuring agreements. Such exemption was given in the form of a new Senate Resolution,[208] and the path was cleared for the continuation of negotiations.

The restructuring agreement concluded between the Government of Brazil and its commercial bank creditors in 1988 contains one example of contractually foreseen renegotiation in the context of development financing involving private sector creditors. It is noteworthy that after conclusion of the 1988 debt restructuring agreement Brazil's external debt obligations with the same universe of creditors were again renegotiated – along the lines of the Brady Plan, as discussed below.

Brazil 1988

The June 1988 restructuring agreement concluded between Brazil and its commercial bank creditors contained a clause providing

---

[208]Senate Resolution, no. 6, dated January 27, 1993.

for renegotiation.[209] Brazil insisted on the inclusion of the clause as a result of internal discussions regarding the impact that fluctuations in external contingencies had on the country's ability to perform its obligations concerning external indebtedness. At the beginning of the negotiations, Brazil actually proposed that interest payments be linked to external contingencies.[210] After long discussions, the parties reached a compromise solution which consisted of a renegotiation clause.

The 1988 restructuring agreement comprised refinancing under four 'new money' facilities, as well as restructuring *strictu senso* under a 'multi-year deposit facility agreement' (MYDFA). Two of the new money facilities were World Bank cofinancing facilities, one of which was a parallel, informal cofinancing agreement, and the second a 'formal' cofinancing, in that disbursements of commercial bank loans were made conditional upon disbursements under related World Bank loans.[211] A third one was a trade deposit facility aimed at providing Brazilian entities with medium-term credits linked to Brazilian import and export transactions. The fourth and final facility provided for the issuance of new money bonds by the Central Bank.

The language on renegotiation was included in the 'miscellaneous' provisions of the term sheet for the agreement, and stated that:

---

[209]On the 1988 Brazil debt restructuring agreement, see Lamdany, Rubem, *The Market-Based Menu Approach in Action: The 1988 Brazilian Financing Package*, 163–174 DEALING WITH THE DEBT CRISIS (I. Husain and I. Diwan editors). Washington DC, World Bank, 1989, 308p.

The 1986 Venezuela restructuring agreement reportedly included a provision along similar lines, the first of its kind to be included in a developing country restructuring agreement. After conclusion of the agreement, the price of oil fell substantially, leading the parties to renegotiate the terms of Venezuela's obligations. Apparently, however, there was no express mention, in the course of negotiations, to the specific renegotiation clause. Interview with Washington DC attorney active in sovereign debt restructuring, September 14, 1990.

[210]Discussions with Central Bank officials.

[211]On the modalities and features of World Bank cofinancing facilities, see Malard, Arielle, LE COFINANCEMENT BANQUE MONDIALE – BANQUES COMMERCIALES, Paris, PUF, 1988, 87p.; Morais, Herbert V., *World Bank Promotion of Private Investment Flows to Developing Countries through Cofinancing and other Measures*. 1–37 ICSID REVIEW – FOREIGN INVESTMENT LAW JOURNAL Spring 1988; Taylor, John L., *A Lawyer's View of Developments in World Cofinancing with Private Banks*, 415–448 CURRENT ISSUES OF INTERNATIONAL FINANCIAL LAW (David Pierce, Helena Chan, Frederick Lacroix and Philip Pillai editors, 1985): *Expanded Cofinancing Operations*, World Bank, Cofinancing and Financial Advisory Services, January 1991.

Provision will be made that any party may propose consultations for the purpose of requesting modifications of the Multi-Year Deposit Facility Agreement by amendment, waiver or consent. During any period of consultation, the Multi-Year Deposit Facility Agreement will continue to apply in accordance with its terms. The Multi-Year Deposit Facility Agreement will contain a recital to the effect that any such proposed amendment under such provision shall be based upon any financial, economic or other factors, events or circumstances that the party proposing it deems relevant, including any change in international economic variables.

Individual agreements were later concluded to implement each of the five facilities provided for under the financing plan. The MYDFA, dated September 22, 1988, was entered among the Central Bank as main obligor, the Republic as guarantor, and the banks. It was the actual 'rescheduling' portion of the arrangement, and comprised deposits in respect of principal maturities falling due during the calendar years 1987 through 1993.

The agreement contained a preamble, and then laid down in detail the modification procedure spelled out in the term sheet. The relevant portion of the preamble read as follows:

Preliminary Statements

This Agreement also contains provisions, set forth in Section 12.01 hereof, pursuant to which any party may propose amendments to this Agreement and related consultations among the parties with respect thereto. Any such proposed amendment under said Section 12.01 shall be based upon any financial, economic or other factors, events or circumstances, that the party proposing it deems relevant, including any change in international economic variables.

The detailed clause on renegotiation, set forth in the concluding provisions of the agreement, provided for consultation procedures which could lead to the 'amendment or waiver' of the contract, upon written agreement between the Central Bank, the Republic and a number of banks representing a certain percentage of all creditors; detailed conditions were set forth for any amendment to be effected. The relevant provision of the MYDFA – Section 12.01 – read:

93

Section 12.01. Amendments, Consultation Procedure.

(a) Amendments. No amendment or waiver of any provision of this Agreement, nor (subject to Section 6.02) consent to any departure by the Central Bank or the Guarantor therefrom, shall in any event be effective unless the same shall be in writing and signed by the Guarantor, the Central Bank and

(i) at least 66–2/3% of the Banks, or

(ii) at least 50% of the Banks in the case of an amendment or waiver of, or any consent to any departure from, the terms and conditions of (x) Section 10.01 (other than subsection (c), (d), (h) or (o) thereof or the phrase ' "or in the case of subsection (c), (d), (h) or (o), or more than 66–2/3% of the Banks contained "therein" ') or (y) Section 11.02 . . .

(including, without limitation, by exchange of telexes), and then such waiver or consent shall be effective only in the specific instance and for the specific purpose for which given, provided that no amendment, waiver or consent shall, (A) unless in writing and signed by at least 95% of the Banks, (I) except as noted in clause (B)(II) below, change the percentage of the aggregate unpaid principal amount of the Deposit Accounts which shall be required for the Banks or any of them to take any action hereunder, (II) waive any of the conditions specified in Article VI, (III) reduce the amount of any principal, interest, fee or other amount payable hereunder to any Bank, (IV) postpone any date fixed for any payment in respect of any principal of, or interest on, the Deposit Accounts or other amounts due hereunder, (V) diminish any of the Guarantor's obligations to any Bank under Article IX or (VI) amend or waive any provision of, or consent to any departure by the Central Bank from, Section 2.01, 3.10, 5.02 or 5.03 or of or from this proviso of this Section; and

(B) unless in writing and signed by all the Banks, (I) subject the Banks to any additional obligations or (II) change the percentage of the aggregate unpaid principal amount of the Deposit Accounts which shall be required for the Banks or any of them to take any action under these clauses (B) (I) and (B)(II); . . .

provided, further, that no amendment, waiver or consent shall, unless in writing and signed by the Agent, by a member of the Bank Advisory Committee for Brazil or by a Coordinator in addition to the Banks required hereinabove to take such action (including, without limitation, by exchange of telexes) affect the rights or duties of the Agent, such member of the Bank Advisory Committee for Brazil or such Coordinator under this Agreement.

The different percentages specified in the amendments clause reflected the degree of importance attached by creditors to the specific clauses of the agreement subject to amendment. Hence, Section 10.01, which could be modified under Section 12.01 (a)(ii) by a simple majority of the creditors, contained the events of termination under the agreement. The 95 percent percentage for amendment applied to Article VI, which referred to conditions to the initial credit date – corresponding to a condition precedent to the initial disbursement under a regular loan transaction; to section 5.02, regarding insufficient funds with the Central Bank as obligor under the agreement; and section 5.03, related to the sharing of certain payments.

The specific provision on renegotiation was contained in subsection (c) to Section 12.01, which dealt with a 'consultation procedure':

> (c) Consultation Procedure. It is understood that any party hereto may propose consultations for the purpose of requesting modifications of this Agreement by amendment, waiver or consent; provided that no such modification shall be effective unless made in accordance with Section 12.01 (a) and (b). During any period of consultation among the parties in respect of such proposal or any period while any proposed modification is being discussed, this Agreement shall continue to apply in accordance with its terms.

It is noteworthy that the set of provisions dealing with renegotiation included in the 1988 debt restructuring agreement did not require that the request for adaptation be caused by some specific event beyond the parties' control. Instead, the renegotiation mechanism was open-ended, and provided that the contract would remain in force and unchanged until any modification was agreed upon.

As stated above, after conclusion of the 1988 debt restructuring agreement Brazil's external debt obligations with the same universe of creditors were again renegotiated. Yet, the renegotiation provision agreed to in 1988 was never expressly invoked as the basis for negotiations, a fact which may be interpreted as speaking against the effectiveness of a renegotiation provision crafted in broad terms.

Chapter Six

ADAPTATION CLAUSES
STRICTO SENSU

Adaptation provisions, unlike renegotiation clauses, provide for automatic adjustment of the terms of the agreement in case of supervening circumstances which alter the contractual balance in a substantial manner. The obligation created by adaptation clauses relates not only to procedure, as do renegotiation clauses, but also to substance, in that the parties agree in advance that the terms of the agreement will be modified should circumstances, specified in the contract, occur.

The notion of 'adaptation clauses' provides a general heading which comprises a wide set of mechanisms designed to minimize the effects that subsequent external changes in circumstances have on the contractual balance. The adjustment mechanism provided for under an adaptation clause may be straightforward, and its application simple, as with an interest capping provision. Conversely, it may require participation of a third party in charge, for instance, of determining whether a given triggering event has in fact occurred, or the extent of the modifications to the obligations of a party resulting therefrom, as may be the case under a contingency financing provision.

Sanctions regarding a party's obligation under a renegotiation clause may be difficult to enforce, because the very breach of such obligation may be difficult to ascertain. A breach of parties' obligations under an adaptation clause, on the other hand, is usually clearcut, since adaptation provisions will typically define triggering events and the contract modification attached thereto in a more precise manner. This characteristic of adaptation clauses might conceivably make them less palatable to creditors, who might resist the idea of binding themselves in advance to the obligation of adapting the terms of a contract.

In reality, however, practice – assuming the meager precedents available can be termed 'practice' – shows that adaptation clauses are viewed preferably over renegotiation clauses because of the predictability of results that characterizes them. This also means, however, that creditors will only agree to the inclusion of an adaptation clause the foreseeable results of which are clearly not detrimental to their interests.

The following discussion of adaptation clauses will not attempt to set forth a general theoretical framework for adaptation provisions under development financing transactions which, given the great diversity of circumstances, obligations and contractual modifications involved, would necessarily be too general, and therefore of little practical use. Instead, the following discussion will analyze adaptation clauses according to the identity of the parties – creditors or debtors – whose obligations are subject to the adaptation mechanism, and according to the nature of the changes the adaptation provision contemplates. The discussion will analyze specifics of such mechanisms according to their relevance to each particular type of clause.

First, provisions entailing adaptation of the obligations of borrowers will be surveyed. This will be followed by discussion of provisions adjusting lenders' obligations.

Adaptation of borrowers' obligations

Adaptation of borrowers' obligations will be analyzed according to the nature of the changes involved. Provisions aimed at reducing interest rate risk will be discussed first, followed by discussion of provisions which link payment obligations to capacity to pay.

Provisions reducing interest rate risk

The developing country debt crisis of the 1980s demonstrated that the burden represented by interest payments under floating rate instruments proved excessive for most debtors. Granted, the actual increase in international interest rates was unusually dramatic, by historical standards, during the period which marked the beginning of the crisis, as discussed in the Introduction to this study, and this factor undoubtedly accounted for a considerable part of the shock. The fact remains, however, that the instruments which evidenced developing country external indebtedness – the syndicated loan agreements – provided no cushion whatsoever to debtors under such changed circumstances. On the contrary, the floating interest rate structure of such instruments dramatically increased borrowers' vulnerability to fluctuations in market interest rates.

The prime source of interest rate predictability is of course the contracting of fixed-rate debt. The fact that the external debt profile resulting from the latest debt restructuring exercises concluded by the major developing country debtor countries is in fixed rate form – more specifically, in the form of a collateralized fixed rate par bond, as discussed above in connection with the Brady restructuring agreements – is very significant in this regard. In practice, this means a large portion of such countries' external indebtedness is protected against interest rate fluctuations.[212]

In addition, hedging against interest rate fluctuations can be achieved by resorting to market-based instruments, as discussed in Chapter 1 to this study. The obstacles to the widespread use of such instruments by official debt managers, also discussed above, underlie the importance of building interest rate protection mechanisms into the agreements themselves.

The set of provisions discussed in the following presents, as a common feature, the fact that they aim at predictability as regards debtors' obligations to service interest under external indebtedness.[213] Parties to a floating interest rate debt instrument loan agreement or bond may stipulate a ceiling to the interest due under the loan, thereby putting a cap on the agreed rate of interest. The excess of the market interest rate over the contractually agreed ceiling can be foregone outright, in which case it amounts to interest capping *strictu senso*; or it can be capitalized,

---

[212]Although not from real interest rate fluctuations. A former director for international affairs with the Central Bank of Brazil underlines the fact that effective protection against interest rate fluctuations would have to take into account the real component of interest rates, taking inflation into account. Accordingly, he conceives a mechanism whereby the rate of interest would be determined *ex post*, discounting the inflation rate for the relevant period; interview with Armínio Fraga Neto in New York, January 25, 1993.

Bergstein, Cline and Williamson discuss a mechanism whereby a cap equal to the real interest rate would be agreed to, with an amount of interest equal to the inflation rate being capitalized. Bergstein, BANK LENDING, at 151–154.

[213]On interest smoothing provisions in general, see BANK LENDING – THE POLICY ALTERNATIVES pp. 133–159.

in which case the provision is an interest capitalization clause.[214] Interest capitalization is clearly a more workable proposition than outright interest capping in the context of voluntary financing transactions.

Interest capping provisions   Under an interest capping clause, parties to a financing transaction agree to subject a floating rate

[214]Prior to the developing country crisis of the 1980s, provisions dealing with interest rate burden had been agreed to in the aftermath of the Second World War under the 1945 *Financial Agreement between the Governments of the United States and the United Kingdom*, under which the United States extended to the United Kingdom a line of credit of $3,750,000,000 designed to 'facilitate the purchases [by the United Kingdom] of goods and services in the United States' (Section 3 of the Agreement, done on December 6, 1945; TIAS 1545.)

The arrangement provided for interest rate waiver in years where the United Kingdom's economy did not fare well. The International Monetary Fund was designated the party responsible for certifying that the triggering event provided for had materialized; this bears a parallel to the role of the Fund under the Mexican value recovery scheme, discussed below.

Section 5 of the Agreement provided:

Waiver of interest payments. In any year in which the Government of the United Kingdom requests the Government of the United States to waive the amount of interest due in the installment of that year, the Government of the United States will grant the waiver if:

(a) the Government of the United Kingdom finds that a waiver is necessary in view of the present and prospective conditions of international exchange and the level of its gold and foreign exchange reserves *and*

(b) the International Monetary Fund certifies that the income of the United Kingdom from home-produced exports plus its net income from invisible current transactions in its balance of payments was on the average over the five preceding calendar years less than the average annual amount of United Kingdom imports during 1936–1938, fixed at [sterling pounds] 866 million, as such figure may be adjusted for changes in the price level of these imports.

In 1957 the interest waiver clause in the original 1945 Agreement had to be renegotiated, and was turned into an interest deferral mechanism. The amended provision amounted to interest capitalization in the sense discussed below, coupled with deferral of principal. The relevant portion of the amended provision read:

Deferment of annual installments

(i) In any calendar year after December 31, 1956, in which the Government of the United Kingdom advises the Government of the United States that it finds that a deferment is necessary in view of the present and prospective conditions of international exchange and the level of its gold and foreign exchange reserves, the Government of the United Kingdom may defer the payment of the annual installment for that year of principal repayment and interest specified under Section 4. Not more than seven annual installments may be so deferred.

(*Agreement to Amend the Financial Agreement of December 6, 1945*, done on March 6, 1957; TIAS 3962.)

of interest to a ceiling, with the excess of the market rate over the agreed ceiling – the interest overage – being foregone.

To the extent interest capping provisions contain an element of concessionality, through the forgiving of the interest overage, such clauses are clearly not a workable proposition in the context of normal, voluntary lending by commercial banks to developing country borrowers, for the obvious reason that creditors cannot be expected to work at a loss as a result of provisions of the loan agreements under which they lend. The same reasoning applies to financing through floating interest rate bond issues: investors will simply not be interested in relatively high-risk instruments the yield of which is below what the market could otherwise offer.

To the extent, however, that the uncertainty as to whether the interest cap will actually become effective seems an attractive bet to creditors, interest capping clauses can arguably be adopted in financing transactions on a commercial basis, in exchange for concessions regarding other aspects of the relevant agreements. The bond exchange agreement concluded between Brazil and its foreign private sector creditors in 1991 to clear interest arrears provides one precedent of a contractually agreed interest rate cap.

Brazil 1991

In September 1990 Brazil initiated discussions in New York with a bank advisory committee aimed at renegotiating the country's external debt. At that time the country had accumulated interest arrears as a result of internal regulations limiting the remittance of interest payments abroad to 30 percent of the amounts due, as well as determining that any installments of principal amortization falling due be deposited with the Central Bank.[215]

Before entertaining proposals for the renegotiation of the principal of the debt, Brazil's creditors insisted that the interest arrears be cleared first. As a result, agreement on the principal of the debt, reached in July 1992 – and described later in this study – was preceded by an interest arrangements package,

---

[215]Remittance of interest was restricted pursuant to Brazilian National Monetary Council Resolution no. 1564 of 1989, and Central Bank regulations issued thereunder.

reached on April, 1991, which featured an interest capping provision.

Before agreeing to the inclusion of the cap, Brazil's creditors suggested that the Government buy the protection against interest rate fluctuation in the market-place, through an interest rate swap. The suggestion was dismissed given the significant amount of debt involved. Creditors eventually agreed to a cap which proved largely comfortable for them, and gained as part of the bargain an option as to interest rate under the instrument which subsequently proved uninteresting for Brazil, as discussed below.

Under the agreement, an amount close to $9 billion worth of interest arrears was restructured. Cash payments were made in the amount of $2 billion, with the balance of the claims being exchanged for bearer bonds with a tenor of ten years and a grace period of three years, with semi-annual principal and interest payments.

As regards interest rates under the bonds, creditors were offered two options – Series A and Series B. Series A bondholders were to receive fixed rates pursuant to an increasing scale through the first three years, and LIBOR plus a margin thereafter.

It was under the second option offered to creditors that a provision for interest ceiling – coupled with an interest floor – appeared. Series B bondholders would receive LIBOR plus a margin; during the first five years, however, the interest rate paid was subject to a floor of 6 percent per annum, and a step-up ceiling of 7.2 percent for the first year, 7.7 percent for the second year, and 8.2 percent for the third, fourth and fifth years. From the sixth year on, the interest rate shall correspond to LIBOR.

The Bond Exchange Agreement among República Federativa do Brasil, Citibank, NA as Closing Agent, and the universe of creditor institutions, providing for the issuance of the bonds in exchange for the interest claims, was dated as of September 10, 1992. A first exchange date, with the related issuance of bonds, occurred in November 1992, and a second one in March 1993.[216]

---

[216]It was agreed under Section 2.04 of the Bond Exchange Agreement that a second exchange date would take place in order to take care of claims which were either unreconciled, or with respect to which the required percentages of waivers under the original loan agreements had not been obtained, by the time of the first exchange date.

The Terms and Conditions of Bonds, endorsed on the bond indenture, provide with respect to interest rate:

3. Rate of Interest

(a) (i) The rate of interest on the Bonds (the 'Rate of Interest') for any Interest Period (as hereinafter defined) shall be * [7–13/16% per annum from January 1, 1991 through (and including) December 31, 1991, 8–3/8% per annum from January 1, 1992 through (and including) December 31, 1992, 8–3/4% per annum from January 1, 1993 through (and including) December 31, 1993, and thereafter,] a rate per annum equal to the sum of (a) 13/16% and (b) the LIBO Rate ** [provided, however, that through (and including) December 31, 1995, if the LIBO Rate for any Interest Period would otherwise be less than the Floor Rate for such Interest Period, the LIBO Rate shall be deemed to be equal to the Floor Rate for such Interest Period, and if the Libo Rate for any Interest Period would otherwise be greater than the Ceiling Rate for such Interest Period, the Libo Rate shall be deemed to be equal to the Ceiling Rate for such Interest Period. 'Floor Rate' means, from January 1, 1991 through (and including) December 31, 1995, 6% per annum. 'Ceiling Rate' means, from January 1, 1991 through (and including) December 31, 1995, the following rates: 7.2% from January 1, 1991 through (and including) December 31, 1991; 7.7% per annum from January 1, 1992 through (and including) December 31, 1992; and 8.2% from January 1, 1993 through (and including) December 31, 1995].

* Series A-L and Series A-U Bonds only.
** Series B-L and Series B-U Bonds only.[217]

As it turned out, the interest caps under Series B bonds never took effect, since market rates for the relevant periods, at historical lows, never reached the agreed levels. In fact, virtually all banks chose Series A bonds, which featured interest rates well above the then prevailing market rates. A few banks did choose Series B bonds, which were however never issued because the minimum issuance thresholds established under the agreement were not reached.[218]

[217]L and U refer to listed and unlisted bonds.
[218]Section 1 (b) of the IDU Bond Fiscal Agency Agreement dated as of September 10, 1992 between República Federativa do Brasil and Morgan Guaranty Trust

Interest capitalization Interest capitalization clauses seek to stabilize interest payments over time, allowing for cash flow predictability, by providing that whenever market interest rates exceed a contractually agreed ceiling, such excess be added to capital, and accordingly be repaid pursuant to the agreed amortization schedule.[219]

In the following, provisions for interest capitalization included in the Brazil 1993 debt restructuring agreement with its foreign private sector creditors will be reviewed.[220] The rationale for the inclusion of the interest capitalization feature was linked to the aim of providing Brazil with cash flow relief in the initial years of the agreement, and this was reflected in the manner the interest capitalization structure was tailored.[221]

Company of New York provided that:

> [the Issuer] shall have no obligation to issue any Series of IDU Bonds which as of the First Exchange Date would have an aggregate principal amount outstanding on the First Exchange Date (including the aggregate principal amount of Unreconciled Bonds of such Series proposed to be issued) less than US $100,000,000.

[219]Because they provide the borrower with temporary cash relief, interest capitalization provisions have been described as 'liquidity caps'; see Griffith-Jones, *Ways Forward*, at 45. For different modalities of interest capitalization, see Hurlock, *Interest Rate Caps*, at 544–546.

For a detailed discussion of the advantages of interest capitalization clauses, as well as of the constraints on their adoption, see Bergsten, BANK LENDING. In particular, the study discusses a suggestion for a 'reimbursable interest-averaging cap':

> The Reimbursable interest-averaging cap (RIAC) is a mechanism that would specify a ceiling for current interest payments. If the normal terms of the loan (for example, LIBOR or prime plus a given spread) exceeded this ceiling because of a rise in international interest rates, the excess due in interest payments would be added to the principal outstanding on the loan. If subsequently international interest rates declined such that the basic loan rate fell below the ceiling, the debtor would continue to pay current interest at the ceiling rate until such funds as had been previously deferred from interest into principal were exhausted. Thereafter current interest would revert to the basic loan terms (market reference rate plus spread). If instead interest rates remained high, interest deferred into principal would become reimbursable at the final maturity of the loan, either in a 'balloon' payment or staged over an additional period.

Bergstein, BANK LENDING, at 133–134.

[220]Reportedly, the 1990 Nicaragua debt restructuring agreement contained a provision regarding interest capitalization whereby interest payments were capped at a rate of 7%, with the excess added to principal outstanding; Bergstein, BANK LENDING, at 154, quoting THE NEW YORK TIMES, December 14, 1982.

[221]In that regard, both the par and the front-loaded interest reduction bonds also contained in the menu of options, as described below, are designed to allow for

For an interest capitalization provision to be acceptable to creditors under a voluntary lending transaction, it would probably have to be coupled with enhancements for creditors, such as an increase in the contractual rate of interest upon the occurrence of the capitalization. Also, the discussion of interest capitalization would probably make more sense in regard to an instrument of relatively short term, since the receipt of the capitalized interest would in such case be a concrete prospect for creditors.

Agreement on an interest capitalization scheme would in any case be acceptable only to the extent that creditors perceived the relevant obligor to be fundamentally creditworthy, but contemplated market circumstances under which it would make sense to grant such obligor liquidity relief through the capitalization of interest. It is submitted this is not an entirely unrealistic scenario.

In any case, it would be an interesting task for financial engineers to devise an instrument embedding an interest capitalization mechanism which is financially attractive to the debtor and its creditors alike. As regards legal technicians, the provisions described in the following demonstrate that the result of their work can help implement whatever the outcome of financial engineering is.

Brazil 1993

After reaching agreement on interest arrears, as described above, Brazil and the bank advisory committee reached an agreement on the restructuring of the country's medium- and long-term public sector debt in July 1992. The term sheet for the deal was concluded in September 1992, and dated as of December 29, 1992, date of publication of the Brazilian Senate Resolution which authorized the Executive Power to conclude the implementing agreements.[222] The implementing agreements providing for the issuance of the bonds and for the payment mechanics thereof were dated as of November 29, 1993, and the bonds issued on April 15, 1994.

---

cash flow relief, through the adoption of a 'step-up' interest rate structure, designed to provide Brazil with alleviated cash flow in the early years of the agreement.

[222]The Brazilian Federal Constitution (article 52) confers upon the Federal Senate the power to authorize the Executive to enter into any agreement of a financial nature involving the Brazilian State.

An example of a debt restructuring agreement along the lines of the Brady Plan, Brazil's agreement comprised elements of debt and debt service reduction, through the exchange of eligible claims for floating interest rate discount bonds and fixed rate par bonds, both collateralized with respect to principal, as well as with respect to twelve months of interest payments. Under the terms of the agreement, collateral for the par and discount bonds, as well as for interest payments under the front-loaded interest reduction bond, were to be delivered over a two-year 'phase-in' period. This novel feature of the deal, which took Brazil and its creditors long negotiating efforts, was necessary because of the impossibility that Brazil deliver all the enhancements on the exchange date, and was indeed a factor which differentiated Brazil's agreement from previous Brady deals.

In addition to the par and discount bonds, the agreement provided for new financing, through a new money option whereby creditors could exchange their eligible credits for debt conversion bonds with a corresponding new money obligation, to be fulfilled through the subscription of new money bonds. The term sheet further included a 'front-loaded interest reduction bond' ('FLIRB'), which featured a 'step-up' rate of interest until the sixth year, and floating rate thereafter, and interest rate guarantee for the first six years; a capitalization bond; and a restructuring option, under which eligible claims were exchangeable not for a bond instrument, but for a loan agreement with longer maturity and modified interest rate.[223]

Brazil's complex debt restructuring agreement further provided for the exchange of claims related to interest due and unpaid since 1991 through the exchange date for bonds. The interest capitalization provisions appear both under the capitalization bond and the restructuring option.

Brazil's capitalization bond – the 'front-loaded interest reduction with capitalization bond' – has a tenor of twenty years and a grace period of ten years. The term sheet provision on interest rate under the capitalization bond read:

C-Bonds will bear interest at the rate of 8.00% p.a. in the case of C-Bonds denominated in U.S. Dollar and 8–3/8%

---

[223]The loan agreement under the restructuring option did not take effect, because the threshold amount for effectiveness any option under the 'menu', as provided in the term sheet, was not reached with respect to the restructuring option.

p.a. in the case of C-Bonds denominated in Deutsche Mark from the Exchange Date, payable semianually in arrears.[224] On each interest payment date occurring prior to or on the sixth anniversary of the Exchange Date, the principal amount of each C-Bond will be increased by the amount of capitalized interest (for the interest period ending on such interest payment date) equal to the difference between the amount of interest calculated at the applicable rate specified below and the amount of interest calculated at the rate of 8.00% p.a. for C-Bonds denominated in US Dollars and 8–3/8% p.a. for C-Bonds denominated in Deutsche Mark.

Bond Currency	Rate
U.S. Dollar	Years 1–2: 4.00% p.a.
	Years 3–4: 4.50% p.a.
	Years 5–6: 5.00% p.a.
Deutsche Mark	Years 1–6: 5–13/16%[225]

This provision of the term sheet translated into complex language regarding 'rate of interest' in the terms and conditions of the bond, written on the reverse of the bond indenture:

The rate of interest payable from time to time in respect of the outstanding principal amount of the Bonds which is not

---

[224]The debt restructuring agreement between Brazil and its creditors provided that the new instruments could be issued not only in US dollars, but also in German marks, if the required commitment amount is met; and also Sterling pounds, in the case of new money bonds.

[225]The provision in the term sheet regarding the restructuring option, in turn, read:

Restructured Credits shall bear interest at the interest rate per annum set forth below:

Credit Currency	Rate
US Dollar	Years 1–2: 4.00% p.a.
	Years 3–4: 4.50% p.a.
	Years 5–6: 5.00% p.a.
Deutsche Mark	Years 1–6: 5–13/16% p.a.

Thereafter, Restructured Credits in each Credit Currency will bear interest on a floating basis at a rate per annum equal to 13/16% per annum plus the six-month LIBO Rate for such Credit Currency. On each interest payment date during the first six years after the Exchange Date, the difference of (i) 13/16% per annum plus the six-month LIBO Rate for each Credit Currency *minus* (ii) the applicable rates specified above, will be calculated. If such difference is positive, Brazil will pay an amount in cash calculated at such applicable rate, and such difference will be capitalized. If such difference is negative, Brazil will pay an amount in cash calculated at such applicable rate, and such difference shall be deemed a prepayment to reduce the aggregate outstanding principal amount of Restructured Credits.

overdue (the 'Rate of Interest') shall be 4.00% per annum from April 15, 1994 through April 15, 1996, 4.50% per annum from April 15, 1996 through April 15, 1998, 5.00% per annum from April 15, 1998 through April 15, 2000, and thereafter 8.00% per annum. The interest payable in respect of the Bonds shall be calculated per each US $1,000 (the 'Minimum Multiple') face amount of Bonds (based on the outstanding principal amount of a Bond having a face amount equal to the Minimum Multiple) and rounded to the nearest cent (half a cent being rounded upwards). The interest payable at any time in respect of any Bond shall be calculated by multiplying the amount of interest payable per Minimum Multiple (calculated as provided above) by a fraction, the numerator of which is the face amount of such Bond (in the case of a definitive Bond) or the original principal amount of the Bonds evidenced thereby at such time (in the case of a Global Bond) and the denominator of which is the Minimum Multiple).[226]

The provision then went on to specify that a 'reference amount' was to be calculated, through the adoption of a scale, the effect of which was to increase the amount in respect to which interest would be calculated during the first six years of tenor of the instrument, thus attaining the capitalization effect.

The set of provisions adopted under LDC debt restructuring agreements, reviewed above, demonstrates that interest rate risk, one of the main sources of difficulties for debtors under transnational lending, can be coupled with through the very terms of the contract, in addition to financial derivatives, discussed in Chap. I of this study.

Provisions linking *obligation* to *capacity* to pay

Fluctuations in international interest rates, a factor which is addressed by the provisions discussed above, are one change in economic/financial variables which directly affects borrowers' obligations under international financing transactions. Past experience demonstrates that in addition to changes having such direct impacts, developing country borrowers' ability to fulfill

---

[226]Different figures applied to instruments issued in German marks.

payment obligations may be equally affected, in an indirect manner, by changes which interfere with their capacity to pay. Examples of such changes are deteriorations in the world price for a key export item, or in a country's terms of trade; or a surge in the price of a major import item for such country, the typical example being oil. When the borrower in question is the developing country itself, such adverse changes usually translate into balance-of-payments difficulties, which imply that the country does not dispose of sufficient foreign exchange to meet its external debt obligations.

The impact that changes in external factors may have upon a borrower's capacity to fulfill obligations under external financing transactions can be conceivably mitigated by the adoption, by the parties to such transactions, of provisions which somehow link obligation to pay to capacity to do so. The most clear instance of one such clause is an indexation provision, under which parties to a financing transaction agree to link payment obligations of the borrower to some measure of its capacity to pay, such as export revenues from a key commodity. Because it explicitly links payment obligations to actual capacity to make payments, outright indexation is arguably the most direct hedging device to which a borrower can resort.

Indexation has been much discussed in the economic literature, in particular in connection with analyses of the causes of the developing country debt crisis of the 1980s. Such *ex post* analyses clearly reveal that the lack of any link whatsoever between developing country borrowers' payment obligations to their capacity to pay contributed to the gravity of the crisis.[227] Accordingly, suggestions were made that new debt capital flows to

[227]See Bergstein, BANK LENDING, in particular at 50–55 and 162–169; Griffith-Jones, *Ways Forward*, at 46; and the pioneer study by Harvey, which is particularly interesting because it was written before the onset of the debt crisis:

> The most important innovation needed concerns the rigidity of present debt service, that is, interest payments and repayment of capital. For governments, repayment should be variable, both up and down, according to some measure of capacity to pay; for projects, loans are needed with some of the conditions normally associated with equity, that is, debt service that varies with the surplus or profits of the project. In both cases the average expected return might have to be higher to compensate the lender for the risk that debt service could be lower in some years; but such compensation should be quite small if it is accepted that lenders also have something to gain from avoiding default and rescheduling.

Harvey, *Reducing the Risk*, at 6.

developing countries draw from such experience in order to include protective mechanisms, such as indexation, in novel lending transactions.[228]

The *commodity-linked bond* is the instrument most commonly suggested: interest and/or amortization payments would vary according to the price of a commodity which was a key export item or source of revenues for the borrowing country or corporate borrower in question.[229] A variation to commodity-linked bonds is *trade-linked* bonds, under which interest payments would be linked to a more general measure of the value of the country's exports, rather than to the price of a particular commodity. Such bonds would present the theoretical advantage over commodity-linked bonds of having a closer correspondence between obligation and capacity to pay;[230] this was probably intended by parties to the Uruguay 1990 debt restructuring agreement, discussed below, under which the relevant trigger for the agreed value recovery mechanism was an index related to the trade balance.

Other than explicit indexation, protection from external shocks which interfere with borrowers' capacity to pay can be structured through a transaction involving a derivative, such as a commodity option, at the time of conclusion of the main financing transaction; such market-based possibility was discussed in the introduction to this study. Hence, a commodity exporter con-

---

[228]For a thorough discussion of the desirable structure of renewed developing country bond borrowing, see Lessard, FINANCIAL INTERMEDIATION, at 79–88:

> A major factor contributing to the debt crisis was the coincidence of the rise in debt-service obligations and the decline in the earnings of commodity exports with which to service debts. With commodity-linked bonds, debt-service obligations would have fallen in parallel with commodity prices, thus providing relief from cash-flow difficulties.

Lessard, FINANCIAL INTERMEDIATION, at 84.
[229]Lessard, FINANCIAL INTERMEDIATION, at 83–85.
[230]Lessard, FINANCIAL INTERMEDIATION, at 85–86.
The inconvenience in using the availability of foreign exchange as the chief measure for a country's ability to service external indebtedness was pointed out in a study by Brainard, Lawrence J., *Emerging Market Sovereign Debt. A New Evaluation Framework*, New York, Goldman Sachs, Emerging Debt Markets Research, October 4, 1991, 21p. The writer submits the experience of the debt crisis demonstrates that a country's fiscal situation is a more appropriate yardstick of the government's capacity to pay than the volume of its foreign exchange reserves. This is indeed in line with the Brazilian government's approach in the renegotiation of 1991–1993, where the profile of the financial instruments was conformed to the government's projected cash flow.

tracting a fixed interest rate financing transaction can hedge against fluctuations in the price of the commodity in question by simultaneously buying a commodity option; if the interest rate under the financing is floating, an interest rate swap could be added to hedge against interest rate risk. Although such transactions have been concluded by some developing country borrowers, they are complex and costly operations which are not, to date, available to most.[231]

As a general matter, lenders would strongly resist subjecting the stream of income they receive under a loan or a bond issue to an unpredictable factor, such as commodity prices. Such reluctance is understandable in light of creditors' interest in assuring a regular and predictable stream of payments.[232]

However, the potential attractiveness of indexed financing to investors in securities and bank lenders has been pointed out in the literature. Higher returns are first and foremost: borrowers would be willing to pay higher yields on such bonds, to compensate for the uncertainty in the repayment stream that the investor would be facing, and for the protection they are deriving against external shocks.[233] In addition, it would be reasonable for indexation mechanisms be conceived so as to work both ways – with payment reductions in times of hardship to the borrower, but also with payment increases in times of windfall gains. Such upward feature of indexed financing – under which a borrower would agree to increase interest payments or to accelerate amortization should circumstances develop in a favorable manner – would be an obvious additional incentive to creditors.[234] Indeed,

---

[231]On precedents, see Masuoka, ASSET AND LIABILITY MANAGEMENT, at 37–42.
[232]As pointed out by Williamson and Lessard:

one can understand the reluctance of financial institutions that issue liquid claims with fixed nominal values (like banks) to place a part of their assets in index-linked bonds that can vary in nominal terms in the short run.

Lessard, FINANCIAL INTERMEDIATION, at 81.
[233]Lessard, FINANCIAL INTERMEDIATION, at 84.
[234]As pointed out by Harvey:

It should not be too difficult to devise a form of lending which allows reduced or zero debt service to be paid in bad years more broadly defined, with compensating higher payments due in good years. Such an arrangement would be more acceptable than a bisque clause, which is simply a concession to the borrower and would thus be unlikely to be agreed to by a wide range of lenders; some compensating accelaration of repayments, in other words 'bisque both ways', would offer something to the lender and thus be more likely to be accepted. It is interesting to notice that accelerated

111

it has been implemented in a few instances in connection with value recovery mechanisms, as discussed in the following.

Direct indexation under mechanisms that link obligation to ability to pay has occurred to a considerable extent in connection with financing transactions involving borrowers from developed countries.[235] It is understandably easier for financial markets to accept such innovative instruments if introduced by borrowers with high credit ratings.[236] Precedents do exist, however, as regards LDC lending, as illustrated in the following section in connection with a performance-linked bond issued by a company from Argentina.

While indexed financing in LDC lending that works to the protection of borrowers features very few precedents yet consolidated, the restructuring agreements along the lines of the Brady Plan have included indexation working in favor of creditors – namely, mechanisms that provide for additional payments to creditors in times of windfall gains to borrowers. The inclusion of such mechanisms, referred to as *value recovery mechanisms or recapture clauses*, is explained by the particular circumstances of the debt restructuring agreements, as discussed below. However, the very fact that such adaptation mechanisms have been conceived, structured and agreed to, underlines the potential for a symmetric use of indexed financing, so as to make it

---

payment in good years might also make it a little easier for countries subject to large fluctuations in foreign exchange earnings to restrain large increases in expenditure in good years, increases which later prove extremely difficult to reverse.

Harvey, *Reducing the Risk*, at 7.
[235] As described by Privolos:

[in response] to the appetite of investors eager to participate in the possible upswing of long underperforming commodities and in response to the risk management needs of primary commodity producers – in particular, precious metal producers – commodity linked securities proliferated in the late 1980s. Securities linked to the price of silver, gold and oil were particularly popular with investors. Almost all commodity-linked financings were issued by corporations and governments in the developed world.

Privolos, *Experience with Commodity-Linked Issues*, at 11.
[236] Lessard, FINANCIAL INTERMEDIATION, at 86.
Official support for novel bond issues, such as the guarantee transactions contemplated under the World Bank's Expanded Cofinancing Operations program, would amount to an important incentive to investors. Indeed, the first transaction under the program involved a guarantee to a $100 million fixed-rate private placement by the House Development Finance Corp. of India. *First ECO Goes to India*, LDC DEBT REPORT July 9, 1990, at 4.

work to the protection of borrowers as well. It is in light of this potential for the conception of symmetric indexation provisions that the value recovery mechanisms will be discussed below.

Before proceeding to the analysis of performance-linked bonds and recapture clauses, it is relevant to note that the inability of a developing country borrower to make payments and be discharged of its contractual obligations under a transnational financing transaction may result, in addition to hardship in connection with changed circumstances, from illegality in connection with subsequent intervening government regulations. Developing country bond issues have featured provisions which are targeted at such situations. While such cases do not characterize adverse changes in circumstances in an economic sense and will not be discussed in the following, they constitute an important device which is available to a developing country borrower seeking contractual protection from subsequent changes.[237]

The following 'dollar constraint' provision, included in the terms and conditions of a fixed rate notes issue by a Brazilian borrower in a transaction which features a trustee, is an illustration of such a clause:

Dollar Constraint. If, after receiving notice from the Issuer or any Noteholder stating that in the Issuer's or such Noteholder's opinion, as the case may be, a Dollar Constraint (as defined in the Trust Deed) has occurred and will affect payment on any Note, the Trustee shall, if it so determines, give notice to the Noteholders that a Dollar Constraint has occurred and that it shall remain in force for such period as is specified in the notice to Noteholders. While a Dollar Constraint remains in force any Noteholder or Couponholder may elect in its sole discretion to receive such payment in the lawful currency of Brazil. In order for such an election to be effective such holder shall at least 15 days prior to the due date for payment deliver to the Issuer, the Trustee and any Paying Agent a notice (a 'Notice') in the form obtainable from any Paying Agent, together with (in the case of the Notice given to such Paying Agent) all

---

[237]However, for market reasons many managers of bond issues view such protective clauses in an unfavorable light, and an issuer may find difficulties fighting for its inclusion in the relevant documentation.

Notes, in the case of any payment of principal, and, in respect of payments of interest, all Coupons as are listed in such Notice.

(. . .)

An election under this Condition may be withdrawn at any time by notice from the relevant Noteholder to the Issuer, the Trustee and the Principal Paying Agent. Any election hereunder shall apply solely to any payment due on such date for payment in respect of which an election has been made and shall bind all subsequent Noteholders or Couponholders.

For this purpose:–

'Dollar Constraint' means any by-law, regulation, directive or communication imposed or issued by the Government of Brazil or the Central Bank of Brazil or any other competent authority in Brazil imposing foreign exchange controls or other restrictions or any refusal or delay by any such party to act which has the effect of prohibiting, preventing or delaying the remittance of US dollars (whether in respect of principal, interest, any additional amounts payable under Condition 7 or otherwise) to any Paying Agent in respect of the Notes when due.

Performance-linked instruments   The issuance in late 1993 by Gas Argentino SA, an Argentinian company, of US $130,000,000 notes with a tenor of five years constitutes the best illustration to date of documentation evidencing external indebtedness of an LDC debtor which features an express link between obligation to pay and capacity to do so.

The profile of the company and of the area of business in which it is active made the issue attractive to investors. Gas Argentino SA holds a long-term concession for the distribution of gas for the urban area of Buenos Aires, and is the holding company of MetroGas SA, a major gas distributor for the same area. Under the structure of the transaction, the notes pay a fixed rate of interest, of 7.25 percent per annum; and an additional rate of return, which may reach up to 2.5 percent, in case the income of MetroGas SA attains given thresholds during a pre-specified period.

By purchasing the notes, investors acquired the right to participate in any increase in income experienced by the issuer, through its controlled subsidiary; the debt instruments were accordingly named *Participating Notes*.

The terms and conditions of the notes provide, with respect to interest:

3. Interest

(a) Interest: Each Note will bear interest from and including the Issue Date (. . .) at the rate of 7.25 percent per annum on the outstanding principal amount thereof, payable semi-annually in arrears (. . .).

(b) Additional Interest: Each Note will bear Additional Interest from and including the Issue Date to, but excluding, the Final Maturity Date at the rate per annum calculated in accordance with paragraph (c) below on the outstanding principal amount thereof, payable semi-annually in arrears (. . .).

(c) Rate of Additional Interest: The rate of Additional Interest applicable to each Annual Interest Period (as defined below) (the 'Additional Interest Rate') shall be calculated in accordance with the following formula:

R is equal to the greater of Z and zero;
where:
'Z' is equal to the lesser of 2.5 and the result of $(X - 85)/15$;
where:
'X' $= AP/BP \times 100$
and where:
'R' is the rate of Additional Interest per annum;
'AP' is the net income of MetroGas for the financial year ended during such Annual Interest Period before income and assets tax, financial and holding results and extraordinary and exceptional items, as determined under MetroGas' audited financial statements and as calculated by reference to the same accounting policies, principles and reporting practices as are adopted in relation to the audited financial statements of MetroGas for the six months ended June 30, 1993 and translated into US dollars by reference to the Conversion Rate at the close of business on the last Buenos Aires Business Day in such financial year as certified to MetroGas, and Issuer, the Principal Paying Agent and the

Trustee by the Auditors of MetroGas in accordance with the Trust Deed; and

'BP' is the benchmark annual profits for MetroGas for the financial year ended during such Annual Interest Period as follows:

Financial year ended	Benchmark annual profits for MetroGas (US$)
December 31, 1993	130,000,000
December 31, 1994	137,000,000
December 31, 1995	156,000,000
December 31, 1996	167,000,000
December 31, 1997	182,000,000

The provision on interest further contained a warning to investors to the effect that:

[the] benchmark annual profits set out [above] are included only for purposes of calculating Additional Interest. There can be no assurance that the amounts included in the benchmark annual profits will be realized; actual future results may be materially higher or lower than those shown.

Hence, according to the condition governing interest rate, the effective rate of interest would depend on the income of MetroGas SA. Such income is to be determined, and certified to MetroGas, the Issuer (Gas Argentino SA), the Principal Paying Agent and the Trustee[238] by the 'Auditors' of MetroGas, in accordance with the Trust Deed. 'Auditors' is a defined term under the terms and conditions of the notes which means:

the auditors for the time being of the Issuer or (as the case may be) MetroGas and, if there are joint auditors, all or any one of such joint auditors or, in the event of any of them being unable or unwilling to carry out any action requested of them pursuant to the Trust Deed, means such other firm of accountants as may be nominated by the Issuer or (as the case may be) MetroGas and approved in writing by the Trustee for the purpose.

The issue of *Participating Notes* by Gas Argentino SA was perceived as a relevant precedent of indexed financing for a

[238]The Trustee under the transaction is Bankers Trust Company Limited; and the Principal Paying Agent, Bankers Trust Company.

corporate borrower from an LDC country. It featured the interesting peculiarity of enabling the company to tap funds at a fixed rate of interest which was lower than it would otherwise had to pay to investors, had it not been for the possibility which was offered to creditors to participate in an increase in revenues. In this sense, the 'protection' to the borrower lies in the limitation to the obligation to pay interest at a fixed rate of interest which is below market; the obligation to pay *additional* interest only arises if and to the extent that the debtor performs well. The mismatch between obligation and capacity to pay is thereby avoided.

From the viewpoint of investors, the transaction was palatable precisely because of this possibility to derive additional income from the activities of a debtor which was perceived as creditworthy and with bright business prospects.

Value recovery mechanisms   An ancillary feature of certain Brady restructuring agreements was the adoption of mechanisms whereby incremental payments to bondholders were provided for, under so-called *value-recovery* or *recapture* mechanisms, in case of a marked increase in the debtor country's capacity to pay, as evidenced by an improvement in the country's trade balance or foreign exchange revenues situation.

From a logical viewpoint, the so-called value-recovery mechanisms were linked to the fact that the Brady deals involved debt or debt service reduction, through the exchange of eligible debt for bonds with a discounted face value, or for par bonds paying a fixed rate of interest estimated to be below market levels. Creditors felt it was justified for them to 'recover' some value – which they had lost as a consequence of the debt exchanges – should the indebted country enjoy a marked improvement in its capacity to pay, as indicated by an agreed measure.

Debtors could contend that debt and debt service reduction is of the essence of a restructuring agreement under the Brady Plan; according to this reasoning, adoption of a value recovery mechanism designed to allow banks to recapture some of the reduction would defeat – it could be submitted – the purpose of the agreement.

Debtors and creditors are unlikely to agree ultimately on

whether debt and debt service reduction was indeed an indispensable element of a Brady restructuring agreement, and practice showed that the issue can only be sorted out in the process of negotiations.[239]

In any case, in the context of voluntary financing unrelated to a debt restructuring exercise, the provision for incremental payment to creditors in case of increased foreign currency revenues would only be arguable in the context of 'base' interest rates lower than market levels, as in the case of the issue by the Argentinian company described above; or in conjunction with a symmetrical mechanism providing for a reduction in payments in case of adverse shifts. Any such two-sided indexation mechanism has apparently remained unexplored to date.[240]

While the various value recovery schemes adopted in country restructuring agreements present certain differences from one another, all bear a common central feature. In essence, a value-recovery mechanism provides for contingency payments to be made by the debtor to the creditors under an instrument – a value recovery right or warranty – attached to the instrument evidencing the country's external indebtedness which materialized the debt or debt service reduction – a par or a discount bond, or both – on the payment dates thereunder.

The right for the additional payments is triggered once an improvement in the country's capacity to pay is characterized. Such an improvement is evidenced by an increase in the country's export revenues, trade balance or GNP. The mechanism requires agreement between the debtor country and its creditors

[239]Hence, the creditors' proposal for the inclusion of a value recovery mechanism in the Brazil 1993 financing package was eventually dropped by creditors themselves upon Brazil's insistence that any value recovery mechanism would only be entertained if some protection against downside risks was also included in the package.

Under Brazil's 1988 Constitution, the Federal Senate has exclusive authority to approve external financial transactions involving the public sector. The Senate Resolution which approved the restructuring agreement concluded with Brazil's private sector foreign creditors in December 1992 provided, under article 9, that the implementing agreements shall in no event provide for recapture clauses, or any other clause which might result in Brazil's creditors recapturing the discount resulting from the negotiation. Article 9 of Senate Resolution 98, of December 29, 1992.

[240]A mechanism on broadly similar lines was contained in the Mexico 1986–1987 agreement, which provided both for contingency financing and for reduction in commitments in case of windfall oil revenues; this mechanism will be reviewed below in connection with adaptation of lenders' obligations.

upon the relevant source of incremental revenues as well as a triggering level; the appointment of a calculation agent responsible for determining, on each payment date, whether the trigger has been reached, and the amounts of the relevant payments, if any; limitations to the payments, as well as suspension or cancellation thereof under certain circumstances.

The natural case for a value recovery mechanism would seem to be that of a country which derives its foreign exchange revenues from one single main export item. The fact that the restructuring agreements of Mexico, Venezuela and Nigeria – major oil-exporting developing countries – all featured value recovery mechanisms seems to confirm this. However, the Uruguay financing plan of 1991 also contained a value recovery mechanism, where the relevant trigger was a commodity terms of trade index which measures the revenues from exports of rice, beef and wheat against the costs of importing oil, resulting therefore essentially in a measure of the country's trade balance. In addition, a value recovery mechanism was included in the Costa Rica financing plan which linked incremental payments to a growth in gross domestic product. Both examples seem to indicate that an indexation provision can be conceived around a more general triggering event.

As regards documentation, a comparative survey of the relevant provisions in the Mexico, Venezuela, Uruguay and Nigeria deals – and Costa Rica's to a lesser degree – reveals a distinct similarity – yet a testimony to the marked standardization of documentation in connection with sovereign debt restructuring.[241] The principal terms of the mechanism, spelled

[241]This standardization in documentation regarding sovereign debt restructuring is described by one author:

> It would be incorrect to suppose that any trend toward an increasing standardization of the documentation for sovereign debt restructurings results entirely from a considered and rational judgment by the parties concerned that a particular format is the most effective way of dealing with the task. There may be a more human explanation for this phenomenon. Many large international banks sit on the steering or advisory committees for a number of sovereign debt negotiations and they are often represented on those committees by the same bank officers. Similarly, the community of lawyers around the world actively engaged in sovereign debt workouts is surprisingly small. (...) Given the natural human instinct to follow precedents when confronted with new and complicated assignments (an instinct with which lawyers are generally thought to be hopelessly afflicted), an increased standardization in documentation relating to sovereign debt restructuring is probably inevitable.

out in the term sheet, are set out in detail in the ensuing documentation. Hence, the exchange agreement generally provided for the issuance, on an anticipated exchange date, of value recovery rights attached to the par or discount bonds being issued in exchange for the outstanding debt. The mechanics of the incremental payments are spelled out in detail in the 'terms and conditions' endorsed on the instrument.[242]

In all instances reviewed, the value recovery rights were issued in registered form, and negotiable separately from the underlying par or discount instrument or note. The terms and conditions of the value recovery rights further contain provisions on aspects such as taxation, transfer and meetings of holders, as well as a choice of law clause for the laws of the State of New York, and English law in the case of Nigeria, a submission to the jurisdiction of courts of New York City and the High Court of Justice in England – in the case of Uruguay, New York courts only, appointment of process agent and waiver of immunities.

It remains true that while the central and common features are those described above, the documentation is complex and varies in several regards. Hence, due to securities law concerns, the rights, as well as the bonds themselves can be issued in the form of a temporary global bond, with the beneficial interest therein being subsequently exchanged for a definitive instrument. Given the fact that payments under the instruments are related to the price of given commodities, provisions directed at complying with commodity regulations are also typically included in the documentation. In addition, specific arrangements are made in connection with the issuance of rights attached to bonds denominated in currencies other than the US dollar. These miscellaneous aspects will not be addressed in the following discussion.

Walker, Mark A., and Buchheit, Lee C., *Legal Issues in the Restructuring of Commercial Bank Loans to Sovereign Borrowers*, 459–474 INTERNATIONAL BORROWING. NEGOTIATING AND STRUCTURING INTERNATIONAL DEBT TRANSACTIONS (Daniel D. Bradlow editor), Washington DC, International Law Institute, 2nd edition 1986, 499p.

[242]Terminology has varied. The instruments evidencing the right for the incremental payments were termed 'value recovery rights', 'value recovery warranties', 'oil-indexed obligations' or 'oil-indexed certificates'.

Mexico 1989

The Mexico 1989 Financing Plan was the first developing country debt restructuring agreement to be reached under the aegis of the so-called Brady Plan. The term sheet for the agreement was dated September 15, 1989, and implementing agreements were signed in early 1990.[243] The agreement involved the exchange of outstanding debt for par and discount bonds, as well as the provision of new money.

The package included a mechanism whereby banks would receive payments under a value recovery right attached to the discount and par bonds, and separately negotiable after a specified date. The value recovery payments shall be in an aggregate amount equivalent to 30 percent of the aggregate incremental oil revenues earned by Mexico. In order to determine this figure the actual revenues are measured against a reference oil price of US $14 a barrel, adjusted yearly for US inflation. Such incremental oil-related payments are subject to an annual limit of 3 percent of each individual bank's eligible claims at the time the agreement was reached, as well as to a limit based on the average oil production by Mexico.

The relevant provision in Part I ('Debt and Debt-service Reduction Options') reads as follows:

From July, 1996 to December 31, 2019, additional payments (the 'Additional Payments') will be made in respect of the Discount and Par Bonds, payable in US Dollars on each quarterly payment date, in an aggregate amount equal to 30% of an amount determined as follows:
(Current Oil Price minus Reference Oil Price) times Current Export Volume times 91 days times the Participation Percentage, where
'Current Oil Price' means, for any quarterly payment date, the average price per barrel of oil exported by Mexico (determined by reference to a surrogate price, as described below) during the four calendar quarters ending before such date; and
'Reference Oil Price' means a price of US $14 per barrel

---

[243]For a summary description of the Mexican 1989–1990 restructuring agreement, see El-Erian, Mohamed A., *Mexico's Commercial Bank Financing Package*, 26–27 FINANCE & DEVELOPMENT September 1990; and Hay, REGULATION OF BANKS, at 3–4.

of oil, as adjusted as of the end of the second calendar quarter of each year (commencing June 30, 1990) for US inflation during the four calendar quarters ending before such date;

'Current Export Volume' means, for any quarterly payment date, the average daily Mexican oil export volume for the four calendar quarters ending before such date; and

'Participation percentage' means the percentage of the aggregate principal amount of Eligible Debt on the Exchange Date that is exchanged for Bonds.

The so-called 'additional payments' were subject to two limitations for every payment period, the first one based on an average oil export volume, and the second on the total of each creditor's credits exchanged for the par and discount bonds. The limitations read as follows in the term sheet:

Limitation on Additional Payments: The aggregate amount of Additional Payments made in any quarter shall be subject to the following limitations:
(a) Additional payments for any quarter may not exceed an amount equal to 30% of an amount determined as follows: (Mexico's average gross quarterly oil export revenues for the preceding four quarters minus the Base Revenue Amount) times the Participation Percentage,
where
'Base Revenue Amount' means 1.25 million barrels per day times 91 days times Reference Oil Price.
(b) The Additional Payments made in the 12-month period beginning July 1, 1996 and in each 12-month period beginning on July of each succeeding year may not exceed 3% of the US dollar equivalent of the Eligible Debt exchanged for Bonds (the 'Base Amount') (1.5% of the Base Amount for the final 6-month period beginning July 1, 2019 and ending December 31, 2019). Additional Payments for any quarter may not exceed 0.75% of the Base Amount; and any amount otherwise payable in any quarter (but for such quarterly payment limitation) shall be carried forward cumulatively and available for making payments at any time when there would otherwise have been a quarterly payment of less than 0.75% of the Base Amount. Accordingly, the maximum amount available to be carried forward from the 12-month

period beginning July 1, 1996 and from each 12-month period beginning on July 1 of each succeeding year will in no event exceed (x) the Additional Payments earned and paid during such period.

The term sheet for the agreement unfolded into the definitive, implementing agreements. Section 2.06 (c) of the Discount and Par Bond Exchange Agreement dated as of February 4, 1990 provided that 'at its original issue, each Bond (. . .) in definitive form [would] have attached to it a Value Recovery Right, registered in the name of the holder of such Bond, in the Notional Amount specified in Section 1(d) of the Fiscal Agency Agreement'.

The Fiscal Agency Agreement entered between Mexico and Citibank, NA, as Fiscal Agent, in connection with the issuance of the par and discount bonds, provided under Section 1(c), that 'at its original issuance, each Bond [would] have attached to it related Rights of 17 Series (Series A through Series Q), each Right to be registered in the name of the registered holder of such Bond'. Section 1(d) of the same agreement further provided that 'the Rights are to be issued only as fully registered Rights in authorized denominations of US $250,000 Notional Amount and integral multiples of US $1,000 Notional Amount in excess thereof (. . .)'.

In addition to the exchange agreements and to the fiscal agency agreement, the face of the instrument evidencing the Value Recovery Right read:

The United Mexican States ('Mexico'), for value received, hereby promises to pay to the registered holder hereof, subject to the provisions contained herein, payments (the 'Value Recovery Payments') in amounts determined pursuant to the provisions set forth on the reverse hereof.

Given the fact that the restructuring agreement was to give Mexico a few initial years of cash flow relief, it was agreed that no payments under the value recovery rights were due before 1996. Accordingly, the form of the Value Recovery Right for the first series of Rights – adjustable for the ensuing series – provided that:

The Value Recovery Payments, if any, shall be payable on

September 30, December 31, March 31 and June 30 (each, a 'Payment Date') commencing on September 30 1996 (. . .)

The operative part of the mechanism was contained on the reverse of the instrument evidencing the value recovery right, termed 'Terms and Conditions of Value Recovery Rights'.

Section 2 (Payments and Paying Agencies) of the Terms and Conditions provided:

(a) The Person in whose name this Right is registered at the close of business on the record date with respect to any Payment Date shall be entitled to receive a Value Recovery Payment equal to the product of (i) the Notional Amount of this Right and (ii) the Value Recovery Payment for such Payment Date in respect of a Right having a Notional Amount of $1.00. For any Payment Date, the Value Recovery Payment in respect of a Right having a Notional Amount of $1.00 shall be equal to:

(A) the product of (1) a fraction, the numerator of which is one and the denominator of which is $47,845,021,625.00, and (2) the lesser of the Excess Price Revenues and the Excess Base Revenues for such Payment Date (the 'Formula Payment'); *plus*

(B) the Carryforward Amount for such Payment Date;

but in no event more than $.0075 (the *'Maximum Payment'*).

The denominator amount used in the Formula Payment equalled the US dollar equivalent of the principal amount of debt which was eligible for the exchange, other than a few categories of excluded debt specified in the agreement. The concepts of Excess Price Revenues and that of Excess Base Revenues, necessary for the comprehension of the Formula Payment, were defined in Section 12 of the Terms and Conditions of the Rights:

'Excess Base Revenues' means, for any Payment Date, thirty percent (30%) of the amount, if any, by which (i) the average gross revenues (expressed in US Dollars) earned by Mexico from the export of Oil (directly or through a Governmental Agency or sales agent) in the preceding four Calendar Quarters ('Current Oil Revenues'), exceeds (ii) the product of 113, 750,000 (representing the number of barrels of Oil assumed for these purposes to have been exported by Mexico in each calendar quarter in 1989) and the Reference Oil Price for such Payment Date.

'Excess Price Revenues' means, for any Payment Date, thirty percent (30%) of the excess, if any, of the average price per barrel (expressed in US Dollars) of Oil exported by Mexico in the preceding four Calendar Quarters ('Current Oil Price') over the Reference Oil Price for such Payment Date times the average of the number of barrels of Oil exported by Mexico in each of the preceding four Calendar Quarters.

The 'Reference Oil Price' was US \$14 ('representing the price per barrel of Oil in 1989 assumed for these purposes') multiplied by an inflation adjustment factor which the definitions went on to specify. The concept of Carryforward Amount, in turn, which was also extensively defined in the document, related to the fact that there was a quarterly limit to the value recovery payments of 0.75 percent – or 3 percent per year – of the credits held by each creditor; should the calculated payment for any given payment date exceed that limit, the excess amount would be 'carried forward' until it could – limitwise – be paid in a subsequent period.

Section 2(c) of the Terms and Conditions provided for the function of calculation agent in connection with the value recovery payments to be performed by the International Monetary Fund:

2. (c) The International Monetary Fund has agreed to act as calculation agent (. . .) in a letter dated (. . .), substantially in the form of the letter attached to the Discount and Par Bond Exchange Agreement as Exhibit 10 (the 'Calculation Letter'), and in such capacity to calculate the Current Oil Price, the Reference Oil Price, the Current Oil Revenues, the Excess Base Revenues and the Excess Price Revenues for each Payment Date based on information adequate for such purposes furnished to the Calculation Agent by Mexico no later than 30 calendar days before such Payment Date, and to deliver to the Fiscal Agent a Calculation Report (the 'Calculation Report'), substantially in the form attached to the Calculation Letter, no later than 20 calendar days before such Payment Date. Mexico hereby agrees for the benefit of the holders of the Rights to furnish to the Calculation

Agent the information required by paragraph 1 of the Calculation Letter no later than the date set forth therein.

The document further provided for a substitute calculation agent:

(f) In the event that the Calculation Agent fails to make the calculations or deliver the Calculation Reports contemplated in subparagraph (c) above, Mexico will:

(i) as soon as practicable thereafter, deliver to the Fiscal Agent a Calculation Letter signed by the International Bank for Reconstruction and Development or the Inter-American Development Bank or another multilateral financial institution, providing for such multilateral financial institution to act as Calculation Agent and, in such capacity, to make the calculations and deliver the Calculation Reports at the times set forth in such Calculation Letter; and

(ii) if necessary pending the delivery of such a Calculation Letter, make the calculations and deliver the Calculation Reports at the times set forth in the Calculation Letter then in effect.

The evolution experienced in the agreements entered into since the conclusion of the Mexican restructuring demonstrates that the function of calculation agent can be performed by a private party, as discussed below. It would indeed be inappropriate to expect the multilateral financial institutions to intervene in any single international financial transaction involving an indexation mechanism. The IMF's participation as calculation agent in Mexico's 1989 financing plan is understandable in light of Mexico's previous 1986–1987 debt restructuring agreement, which included a contingency financing facility linked to an IMF oil-indexed facility which required IMF intervention anyway, as described below. However, if such mechanisms are to become generalized, they would have to be structured without official intervention.

Venezuela 1990

Venezuela reached a restructuring agreement with its private sector creditors in mid-1990. The term sheet, dated June 25, 1990, provided for the exchange of eligible debt for a combination of collateralized par and discount bonds, a partially collateralized – with respect to interest only – temporary interest reduction bond, and a collateralized short-term discount note. The agreement also provided for the disbursement of new money under a new money option.

The value recovery mechanism, spelled out in the term sheet, provided for oil-indexed payments to be made by Venezuela under Oil-Obligation Certificates, attached to the par and discount bonds, commencing in April 1996. The aggregate amount of payments would be calculated on the basis of the excess of the effective oil revenues earned by Venezuela over a strike price of US $26 per barrel.[244] The calculations under the mechanism are to be made not by the International Monetary Fund – as under the Mexico agreement – but by an international auditing firm.[245] The agreement provided also for suspension of the oil-indexed payments under 'tolling provisions' in case of a decline in Venezuela's oil output due to a specified set of circumstances. A limit of US $3.00 per Oil-indexed Payment Obligation was agreed.

Section 1 of the Discount and Par Bond Fiscal Agency Agreement dated December 18, 1990, among the Republic of Venezuela, Banco Central de Venezuela as the official financial agent of the Republic of Venezuela and the Chase Manhattan Bank, NA as Fiscal Agent provided that:

(a) The Republic has entered into a Discount and Par Bond Exchange Agreement dated as of December 5, 1990 (. . .) providing for the issue by the Republic of Collateralized Floating Rate Bonds due 2020 and the Collateralized Fixed Rate Bonds due 2020 (. . .) and related oil-indexed payment obligations (the 'Oil Obligations') evidenced by the Oil Obligation Certificates (. . .)

(c) At its original issuance, each Bond will have attached to it an Oil Obligation Certificate evidencing related Oil Obligations in the ratio of five Oil Obligations per US $1,000 or the US Dollar equivalent thereof (. . .) of the unpaid principal amount of the Committed Debt exchanged for such

---

[244]The term sheet explained that such strike price reflected a price of 20.5 at the time of conclusion of the agreement, adjusted for inflation by an assumed inflation factor for the first six years, and to be subsequently adjusted on the basis of the US producer price index for finished goods, excluding energy prices.
[245]Espineira, Sheldon y Asociados, a member firm of Price Waterhouse, under a Calculation Agent Letter dated December 18, 1990 to the Republic of Venezuela and Chase Manhattan Bank, NA, as Fiscal Agent, which sets out its duties.

Bond.[246] All Oil Obligations will be denominated in US Dollars (without regard to the currencies of the Bonds to which they are initially attached and the Scheduled Payments for such Oil Obligations may be separately transferred, subject to the applicable restrictions specified in the Oil Obligation Certificates and in Sections 3 and 5.

(d) The Oil Obligations are, except as provided in Section 3, to be issued only as Oil Obligations evidenced by registered form Oil Obligation Certificates in minimum denominations of 1250 Oil Obligations (the 'Authorized Oil Obligation Amount') and integral multiples of five Oil Obligations ('Minimum Oil Obligation Multiple') in excess thereof (. . .) in a denomination equal to the amount of such Committed Debt or such US Dollar equivalent (. . .) divided by US $200.00, and such Oil Obligations may thereafter be transferred in such smaller denomination (. . .).

Section 2(a) of the Terms and Conditions of the Oil-Indexed Payment Obligations, written on the reverse of the Oil Obligation Certificate, provides:

(a) The Person in whose name the Obligations evidenced by this Certificate are registered at the close of business on the record date with respect to the Obligation Payment Date for each Scheduled Payment for such Obligations shall be entitled to receive on such Obligation Payment Date a Scheduled Payment for each such Obligation equal to the excess (if any) resulting from subtracting the Strike Price for the immediately preceding Determination Date from the Reference Price for such Determination Date: provided, that in no event will the Scheduled Payment on any Obligation Payment Date exceed US $3.00 per Obligation.

The concepts used in the payment formula were contained in the section on definitions of the terms and conditions of the certificate:

'Reference Price' means, for each Determination Date, a price per barrel of Crude Oil equal to the Export Revenues for the Determination Period ending immediately prior to such Determination Date divided by the aggregate number of US

---

[246]The concept of Committed Debt referred to the eligible debt tendered for the relevant option.

barrels of crude oil included in the exports of Crude Oil during such Determination Period.

'Export Revenues' means, as of any date of determination for any period, the aggregate for such period of (i) each Export of Crude Oil during such period multiplied by (ii) the Invoiced Price for such Export, adjusted as applicable as provided in the last sentence of Section 3(e) hereof.

'Strike Price' means, for the first Determination Date, US $26.00, and for each Determination Date thereafter, the Strike Price for the immediately preceding Determination Date increased or decreased, as the case may be, by the percentage of change in the United States Department of Labor, Bureau of Labor Statistics Producer Price Index for Finished Goods less Energy (. . .).

The value recovery mechanism was conceived so as to have payments under the oil-indexed obligations suspended upon the occurrence of a decline in Venezuela's production of oil, as caused by a specified set of events. Payments would accordingly be resumed once production returned to normal levels.

Section 5 (*'Suspension of Payments'*) of the terms and conditions of the obligations reads:

(a) Upon the occurrence of a Decline Period, the Republic shall deliver to the Calculation Agent, within 15 days following the last day of such Decline Period, a certificate (i) specifying the Suspension Event that has occurred and certifying that the decline in the volume of Exports of Crude Oil for such Decline Period is a direct result of the occurrence of such Suspension Event and (ii) setting forth the volume of Exports of Crude Oil (expressed in barrels of Crude Oil) for such Decline Period and the volume of Exports of Crude Oil (expressed in barrels of Crude Oil) for the six consecutive six-month periods immediately preceding such Decline Period (. . .).

The clause goes on to provide that the Calculation Agent shall perform audit procedures in connection with the determination of the decline in oil production, deliver to the Fiscal Agent a Suspension Report should it verify that the required decline has indeed occurred, as well deliver a later Resumption Report if and when normal levels of production are resumed.

The relevant concepts for the determination of the suspension of payments are contained in the definitions section:

'Decline Period' means any six-month period ending on the last day of a Determination Period for which the volume of Exports of Crude Oil declines, directly as the result of the occurrence of a Suspension Event, by more than 7.5% as compared to the six-month average of the volume of Exports of Crude Oil for the six consecutive six-month periods immediately preceding the six-month period in question.

'Suspension Event' means any of the following events: acts of God, acts of the public enemy, war (declared or undeclared), civil war, acts of sabotage, acts of piracy, official acts such as blockades and declared embargoes imposed against Venezuela or the location of any storage facilities for Crude Oil held for Export outside of Venezuela by foreign powers, revolution, riot, insurrection, civil disturbance, or terrorism; epidemics, natural disasters such as violent storms, hurricanes, tornadoes, cyclones, tidal waves, landslides, destruction by lightning, earthquake or flood; fires, explosions, destruction of machines, oil extraction facilities, production facilities or factories, and of any other type of oil-related installations; and labor-related disruptions affecting the Venezuelan petroleum industry or the location of any storage facilities for Crude Oil held for Export outside of Venezuela, such as boycotts, strikes, lock-outs of any kind, go-slows, occupation of factories or premises and work stoppages.

Nigeria 1991

Nigeria, another major developing country oil producer, also concluded a debt restructuring agreement with its foreign private sector creditors featuring a value recovery mechanism. The obligor under the restructuring agreement is the Central Bank of Nigeria, with the Federal Republic itself appearing as guarantor. Under the package, banks were offered a combination of a collateralized par bond option, a short-term debt exchange option, and a new money bond option.

The term sheet, dated October 15, 1991, provided that

'Payment Adjustment Warrants' would be issued together with the Par Bonds, and entitle their registered holders to oil-indexed payments, commencing in November 1996, under a mechanism that resembles that of the Venezuela agreement. The reference price in the case of the Nigeria arrangement was US $28 per barrel of a given type of oil, Bonny Light, adjustable by a US inflation index. As was the case under the Venezuela deal, payments were subject to a maximum amount, as well as to a 'tolling' provision should oil production decline as a result of specified circumstances; unlike Venezuela, however, payments are to be cancelled, not merely suspended, under said circumstances. The function of calculation agent is to be performed by Citibank, NA, which is also the Fiscal Agent.

The Exchange Agreement for the Collateralized Fixed Rate Bonds, dated December 20, 1991, provided under Section 2.05 that

> Each Bond issued to a Bank will have attached to it a Warrant evidencing payment adjustment rights ('Payment Adjustment Rights') in the ratio of one Payment Adjustment Right for each $1,000 of principal value of Bonds issued to such Bank provided that no Payment Adjustment Right shall be issued in relation to any fractional amount of a Bond which is less than $1,000.

The payment amount itself was to be determined in accordance with the provisions of the 'Conditions of Warrants'.[247] Section 3 ('Calculation of Payment') of said terms provides:

> (B) Each Warrantholder shall be entitled to receive on a Payment Date in respect of each Payment Adjustment Right to which it is entitled, an amount in Dollars which is equal to the excess (if any) resulting from subtracting the Reference Price for such Payment Date from the Average Price for such Payment Date and multiplying the resultant figure by $5.00 (each a 'Payment Amount') provided that in no event shall a Warrantholder be entitled to receive more

---

[247] The fact that the documentation was prepared by a UK law firm in the case of Nigeria, rather than a US firm, accounts for a few variations in the terminology used – such as payment 'warrants', as opposed to 'rights' or 'obligations'. Also, English law, rather than that of the State of New York, was chosen as the applicable law.

than $15 per Payment Adjustment Right in respect of any Payment Date.

'Average Price' means, in relation to a Payment Date, the average of the BBQ Price during the Determination Period;

'BBQ Price' means the mid-rate between the buy/sell Dollar spot price per barrel shown for BBQ under the heading 'Spot Crude Price Assessments' as set forth in Platt's Oilgram Price Report ('Platt's') on each Business Day during the Determination Date (. . .)[248]

'Determination Period' means, in relation to a Payment Date, each six month period which ends on the day which is sixty days before such Payment Date.

'Reference Price' means, in relation to the November 1996 Payment Date, $28 per barrel. Thereafter 'Reference Price' shall mean $28 per barrel, as adjusted by the percentage of change in the United States Labor Department Unadjusted Producer Price Index for Finished Goods less Energy (or any comparable successor index or measure which is substituted therefor) as set forth in 'The Producer Price Indexes' published by the US Government Printing Office, Washington DC, which most recently precedes the relevant Payment Date.

As regards cancellation of the oil-indexed payments upon a decline in Nigeria's oil output, Section 4 ('Cancellation of Payments') of the Conditions of Warrants provides that:

(A) If as a direct result of the occurrence of a force majeure circumstance referred to below, the average daily production of Oil for a six month period (as determined by reference to 'Oil Market Reports' published by the International Energy Agency (or if not available any comparable publication)) falls below one million six hundred and eighteen thousand and seven hundred and fifty (1,618,750) barrels per day during a Determination Period, then the requirement to make payments under the Warrants (if any) on the Payment Date immediately following the relevant Determination Period will be cancelled in accordance with the provisions of this Warrant Condition ('Cancellation Event').

'Force majeure' means any of the following events: acts of

[248]The definition of BBQ Price went on to provide a substitute BBQ Price should the Platt's Price Report not be available for the relevant determination period.

the public enemy, war (declared or undeclared), civil war, acts of sabotage, acts of piracy, official acts such as blockades and declared embargoes imposed against the Republic by foreign powers, revolution, riot, insurrection, civil disturbance or terrorism, epidemics, natural disasters such as violent storms, hurricanes, tornadoes, cyclones, tidal waves, landslides, destruction by lightning, earthquake, flood or other natural disasters, fires or explosions, and labour-related disruptions materially affecting the Nigerian petroleum industry.

'Oil' means crude oil produced in the Republic (regardless of grade or quality) together with any other associated hydrocarbon liquids combined therewith and condensates.

Since the Cancellation Event was to be ascertained by the Central Bank of Nigeria itself, the Conditions of the Warrants provide for an opportunity for 50 percent of the warrantholders to refer the determination as to whether a Cancellation Event, as defined in said Conditions, has indeed occurred, to an independent expert. If said percentage of warrantholders does choose to call on an expert, the Central Bank, as issuer of the warrants, shall be given the opportunity to withdraw its Cancellation Certificate – that is, a notice to the Calculation Agent to the effect that a Cancellation Event has occurred. If it does not, Section 4(D) of the Conditions of Warrants provides that the matter shall be referred to an expert, to be chosen by the President of the London Court of International Arbitration from a list of names, provided by the Central Bank and the Calculation Agent, composed of experts selected from a list held by the Institute of Petroleum, London.

The Conditions of Warrants further contains provisions governing the work of the expert. Section 4(E) (c) provides that 'if the Expert determines that a Cancellation Event has not taken place, then the Payment Amount in respect of the relevant Payment Date will be due and payable and shall be treated as due and payable as from the date which is five Business Days following the date of such determination'.

Uruguay 1990

Uruguay's restructuring agreement, concluded in November 1990, comprised a cash buyback, whereby eligible debt was redeemed at a discount against cash, the provision of new money under new money notes, and a 'Collateralized Fixed Rate Note Exchange'. 'Value recovery rights' were issued attached to such fixed rate notes, which corresponded to the par bond under other restructuring agreements. The obligor under the new instruments was Banco Central del Uruguay, with the Republic appearing as guarantor.

Unlike Mexico, Venezuela and Nigeria, Uruguay is not a major oil producer, nor does it derive most of its hard currency earnings from any single commodity. Accordingly, the recapture provision under the Uruguay deal was constructed around a commodity terms of trade index which measures earnings from a basket of commodities consisting of wool, beef and rice against the cost of oil imports, so that the relevant indicator for the mechanism is Uruguay's trade balance, as measured by specified items.[249]

As in the deals previously described, the commodity-indexed payments were to commence a few years after the issuance of the instruments, so as not to defeat the attempted cash flow relief in the initial years of the agreement. Indexed payments are subject to a maximum amount. The calculation agent under the mechanism is again Citibank, NA. There is provision for cancellation of payments in case Uruguay suffers adverse shocks affecting its revenues from the export of the relevant commodities.

Annex B of the term sheet for the Uruguay agreement, concerning 'Value Recovery Obligations', provided:

Each Purchaser of Fixed Rate Notes will receive one Payment Obligation of the Issuer for each US $250,000 principal amount of Fixed Rate Notes purchased by it. Each such Payment Obligation will entitle the holder thereof to receive on each Payment Date an amount equal to US $250.00 for each 1.00 by which the Commodity Terms of Trade Index exceeds 110, up to a maximum payment of US $3,750.00 on

[249]This means that Uruguay's obligation to make additional payments under the mechanisms can be theoretically triggered not only by an improvement in its export receipts, but also by a marked decrease in the price of oil.

any Payment Date (except that the maximum for the last Payment Date will be determined in accordance with the number of days in the period between the preceding Payment Date and such last Payment Date); provided, however, that if at any time during the six-month period preceding such Payment Date an Unforeseen Event shall have occurred, the obligation of the Issuer to make any such payment on such Payment Date shall be cancelled.

Definitions

Base Period: The period of thirty-six calendar months ending June 30, 1990.

Base Price: For each Commodity, the arithmetic mean of the Prices for such Commodity for each month in the Base Period.

Business Day: Any day of the year other than a Saturday, Sunday or a public or bank holiday in New York City.

Commodity: Each of Beef, Oil, Rice and Wool

Commodity Terms of Trade Index: For any Reference Period, an amount (rounded upwards to two decimal places) equal to

$(RB.288 \times RW.554 \times RR.158/RO) \times 100$

where

RB = Price Index for Beef for such Reference Period

RW = Price Index for Wool for such Reference Period

RR = Price Index for Rice for such Reference Period

RO = Price Index for Oil for such Reference Period

Payment Date: Semi-annually, beginning 5–1/2 years after the Closing Date, and, with respect to Payment Obligations issued with any Series of Fixed Rate Notes, the Fixed Rate Note Maturity Date for such Series.

Price: For any Commodity and any month, the price that appears for such month in the indicated Reference Source:

Commodity Reference Source

Beef: IMF, International Financial Statistics – Commodity Prices, Beef, United States (New York)

Oil: IMF, International Financial Statistics – Commodity Prices, Petroleum Spot, UK Brent

Rice: IMF, International Financial Statistics – Commodity Prices, Rice, United States (New Orleans)

Wool: IMF, International Financial Statistics – Commodity Prices, Wool

Price Index: For any Commodity in respect of each Reference Period, the arithmetic mean of the Prices for such Commodity for each month during such Reference Period, divided by the Base Price for such Commodity.

Reference Period: In reference to each Payment Date, the thirty-six calendar months ending with the third month immediately preceding such Payment Date.

Unforeseen Events: Acts of God, acts of the public enemy, war (declared or undeclared), civil war, acts of sabotage, acts of piracy, official acts such as blockades and declared embargoes imposed against Uruguay by foreign powers, revolution, riot, insurrection, civil disturbance or terrorism, epidemics, natural disasters such as violent storms, hurricanes, tornadoes, cyclones, tidal waves, landslides, drought or destruction by lightning, earthquake or flood which have a material adverse effect on Uruguay's real revenues deriving from the export of Beef, Wool and Rice.

Section 2.01 of the Collateralized Fixed Rate Note Exchange Agreement dated January 31, 1991 between Banco Central del Uruguay as issuer and Citibank, NA as closing agent provided that on the exchange date each creditor that had committed to purchase the collateralized notes would exchange its Committed Debt for Notes in an aggregate principal amount equal to the amount of its Committed Debt and for Rights representing its Related Amount of Value Recovery Rights for such Exchange Date. The provision went on to specify that 'a Purchaser's "Related Amount" of Value Recovery Units for an Exchange Date is the principal amount of Notes purchased by it on such Exchange Date divided by US $250,000 (rounded, if necessary, downward to the nearest two decimal places)'.

The operative part of the value recovery mechanism was spelled out under the Terms and Conditions of Value Recovery Rights. Section 2 ('Payments') thereof reads:

(a) The Value Recovery Payment payable on this Right on each Payment Date equals the product of (i) the number of Value Recovery Units represented by this Right and (ii) the Value Recovery Payment in respect of one Value Recovery unit for such Payment Date. For any Payment Date, the Value Recovery Payment in respect of one Value Recovery Unit shall be equal to the lesser of (x) the Formula Amount for the Reference Period for such Payment Date and (y) US $3,750.

As regards the 'Formula Amount', the definitions section of the Terms and Conditions of Value Recovery Rights provide that:

'Formula Amount' means, for any Reference Period, US $250 multiplied by the excess, rounded down to the nearest whole number, of the Commodity Terms of Trade Index for such Reference Period over 110, or if there is no such excess, zero.

'Commodity Terms of Trade Index' means, for any Reference Period, the number equal to where B, P, R and W equal the quotient obtained by dividing, respectively, the Reference Price for beef, petroleum, rice and wool by, respectively, the Base Price for beef, petroleum, rice and wool.

'Base Price' for beef, petroleum, rice and wool means, respectively, 85.5, 17.2, 405.5 and 975.1. The Base Price for each such Commodity is the arithmetic mean of the Monthly Prices for such Commodity for the 36 calendar months in the period beginning on July 1, 1987 and ending on June 30, 1990.

Given the long tenor of the value recovery rights, which mature simultaneously with the related fixed rate note – which has a tenor of thirty years, Uruguay's agreement contained a provision on the modification of the reference prices under certain circumstances.[250] The initial reference prices were agreed upon on the basis of prices published in INTERNATIONAL FINANCIAL STATISTICS. Uruguay and its creditors agreed that in case that publication ceased to constitute a suitable source for the reference prices, the Central Bank, as issuer of the rights, shall notify the Fiscal Agent of a new method by which it proposes the reference price be calculated. In case a required percentage of rightsholders disagrees with the issuer on such proposed method, the matter will be referred to an arbitrator. The arbitrator shall be appointed by the President of the Federal Reserve Bank of New York, and shall be 'a person who is familiar with the publishing and

---

[250]Section 10 of the Terms and Conditions of Value Recovery Rights.

quotation of prices of grades of such Commodity and who, in the judgment of the Appointing Official, has no substantial reason to favor the Issuer of the Rightsholders in respect of such determination and adjustment'.[251]

Costa Rica 1989

Costa Rica concluded a restructuring agreement with its commercial bank creditors in the end of 1989. The term sheet, dated December 18, 1989, provided for the cash buyback of eligible debt at a discount, with the exchange of remaining claims for par bonds, issued in bearer form, with a fixed interest rate.

Par bonds were issued in two series. Series A par bonds, guaranteed with respect to interest payments only, would be exchanged for claims of creditors having tendered 60 percent or more of their claims under the cash buyback option; creditors whose voluntary participation in the cash buyback was under 60 percent of their eligible claims received series B par bonds, with longer tenor and grace period than series A bonds, and no interest collateral. Claims related to interest arrears which had accumulated at the time the agreement was concluded were also exchanged for the new instruments under the agreement.

The value recovery payments as conceived under the Costa Rica restructuring plan were conceived be applied to accelerate amortization of the interest arrears bonds, and to constitute additional payments ('bonus payments') under the par bonds. The triggering event under the mechanism is an increase, of at least 20 percent, in Costa Rica's real gross domestic product over 1989 levels. Aggregate payments are subject to a ceiling of 4 percent of the aggregate amount of debt under the par and the interest arrears bonds. Since the interest arrears bonds have shorter maturity than that of the par bonds, once the former are no longer outstanding, the ceiling becomes 2 percent of the aggregate amount of outstanding bearer par bonds.

The working of the value recovery mechanism is thus established in the term sheet:

---

[251]Subsections 10(a) through 10(d)(i) of the Terms and Conditions of Value Recovery Rights. Section 10(d) also provides that in case the Appointing Official does not make the appointment, the Issuer – and upon his failure to do so, the Fiscal Agent – will apply to the Supreme Court, New York County, to appoint an arbitrator.

Commencement: Value recovery payments will be required in each year (each a 'Recovery Year') that Costa Rica's gross domestic product ('GDP') in the immediately preceding calendar year, as reported by the IMF and expressed in US Dollars, exceeds 120% of the 1989 level of GDP in real terms.
Measurement: Subject to the caps set forth below, an aggregate amount in each Recovery Year, payable semi-annually, equal to the amount which, when added to the aggregate interest payable during the immediately preceding calendar year on the Bearer Bonds and Interest Claims, and when such sum is divided by Costa Rica's GDP in such immediately preceding calendar year, will equal the Base Year Ratio.[252]
Base Year Ratio: A fraction equal to the amount of interest accrued in 1990 on Bearer Bonds and Interest Claims (on an annualized basis, as if they were issued on January 1, 1990) divided by Costa Rica's GDP during 1990.
Application: Value recovery payments will be first applied pro rata to satisfy each Interest Claim in inverse order of maturity, and then allocated pro rata as bonus payments in respect of each Bearer Bond.

Hence, like the case of the Uruguay restructuring agreement, the mechanism adopted under Costa Rica's was constructed around a more general measure of the country's capacity to pay. Together with the value recovery mechanisms built into the debt restructuring agreements of Mexico, Venezuela and Nigeria, they constitute examples of provisions adapting – in all cases, upwards – borrowers' obligation to pay to their capacity to do so.

Adaptation of lenders' obligations

In addition to provisions adapting the obligations of borrowers, the adverse impact that changes in circumstances have on their ability to meet payment obligations under transnational financing transactions can also be conceivably remedied or mitigated by the adoption of contractual arrangements adapting *lenders'* obligations to the new, changed setting. Indeed, when

---

[252]Interest Claims is the denomination given under the term sheet to the interest arrears bonds.

the adverse changes result in a liquidity problem occurring in the short- or medium-runs – in connection, for instance, with balance of payments difficulties – the contractual relationship can be preserved by the provision of temporary, contingency financing. Such adaptation of lenders' obligations will be discussed in the following.

Lenders' obligations under a financing transaction consist mainly in the extension of the agreed funds to the borrower, even though more than one modality of disbursement can be agreed, as reviewed above. Disbursement under a loan agreement can be up-front, on a revolving basis, or under a stand-by modality. Disbursements under bond issues are usually made up-front, although underwriting, or subscription agreements, may provide for disbursement in installments, which has indeed occurred in connection with new money bond subscription agreements in the context of Brady restructuring agreements. Flexibility as to timing and amount of disbursement is also ensured through the adoption of so-called 'medium-term note programs' which allow an issue of securities to the borrower as and when required.

Adaptation of creditors' obligations will usually refer to modifications of such disbursement obligations, and, more specifically, of the amount of disbursement. A creditor's obligation to extend funds can be adapted upwards, so as to require additional financing; or downwards, in which case it amounts to a reduction in commitments. Both types of adaptation will be discussed in the following.

Contingency financing

Contingency financing clauses can be structured as a mechanism under which lenders commit to provide additional financing in the event of adverse circumstances that impair the borrower's capacity to service outstanding debt, such as – in the case of a sovereign debtor – a decline in the price for the country's main source of hard currency earnings. From a financial viewpoint, a provision for contingency financing is an indexation clause, the immediate impact of which, however, applies to the obligations of the lender, rather than to the borrower's, as discussed so far.

Contingency financing amounts to contract adaptation to the extent it results in the modification of the amounts of the financing. In an economic sense, contingency lending addresses the problem of liquidity, thereby mitigating the impact that adverse external contingencies have on borrowers' capacity to meet obligations under existing credits; in this sense, they follow the same rationale as interest capitalization clauses, discussed above.[253]

While they have been adopted in the context of involuntary lending in connection with debt restructuring agreements, as described below, as a general matter creditors would be reluctant to agree to contingency financing mechanisms under a voluntary, fresh financing transaction, for the simple reason that creditors would rather stay away from extending additional financing to a debtor under strain. This is illustrated by the difficulties in filling the financial gap in restructuring exercises during the debt crisis, when the refinancing portion of restructuring packages amounted to *ad hoc*, as opposed to contractually foreseen, contingency financing.

Voluntary contingency financing is envisageable, however, if the contingency which triggers the provision is perceived – and contractually defined – not as a dramatic hardship which imperils the debtor' ability to meet its obligations under the financing transaction, but rather as a predictable fluctuation which makes the fulfilling of the debtor's obligation temporarily more burdensome. If coupled with a symmetrical provision for the reduction of commitments in case of an improvement in the situation of the borrower – along the lines of the value recovery mechanisms described above – contingency financing should be all the more palatable to creditors.[254]

While it is theoretically workable in the context of a loan transaction, contingency financing is more difficult to conceive

---

[253]The attractiveness of contingency financing provisions had been pointed out in the pioneer study of Harvey, in 1981:

> An alternative to flexible debt service arrangements is access to additional credit; this is an acceptable alternative from the borrowers point of view, provided that it is secured well in advance, since negotiating additional credit in a crisis is likely to be much more difficult and expensive than an arrangement built into an original finance agreement.

Harvey, *Reducing the Risk*, at 8.

[254]'On balance, contingency lending may be helpful in some cases, especially where a single commodity is dominant, and on a basis symmetrically providing for reduction of new money if the commodity-price increases', Cline, MOBILIZING BANK LENDING, at 32.

and implement under a bond issue. One could possibly conceive an initial subscription above the financing initially required, with the overage to be set aside in a pool from which resources could be drawn under certain pre-specified circumstances.[255] Alternatively, contingency financing through the issuance of bonds could be structured by providing in the applicable subscription agreement that the relevant universe of creditors shall be under the obligation to subscribe to a supplemental issue by the borrower, in case a pre-specified contingency materializes.

The Mexican restructuring package of 1986–1987 contains a precedent of a contingency financing mechanism.[256]

Mexico 1986–1987 The 1986–1987 Commercial Bank Financing Package for Mexico comprised both restructuring and refinancing.[257] It consisted of amendments to the credit agreements entered into by the central government in 1983 and 1984, as well of amendments to 52 'restructure agreements' and to 35 'new restructure agreements' entered by public sector obligors. The refinancing portion consisted of four new money financing facilities. Two of the new money facilities were credit agreements parallel to World Bank sectoral loans, in the total amount of US $6 billion. The two remaining facilities were contingent facilities: one 'growth-related contingency financing' with the World Bank in the amount of US $500 million, and a 'contingent investment support financing' in the amount of US $1.2 billion.

Implementing agreements were subsequently concluded. The refinancing facilities, including the two contingency financing facilities, were the object of a single, multi-facility agreement

[255]Interview with official from major commercial bank with headquarters in New York; January 25, 1993.
[256]A similar mechanism was reportedly also thought of under the Mexico 1989 restructuring, but eventually dropped:

> A contingent financing facility to be called in the event of lower than expected oil prices (with a proposed World Bank guarantee feature) was agreed in principle by a limited number of major creditors, but was never concluded.

Hay, REGULATION OF BANKS, at 4.
[257]While the following discussion is based on primary materials, the contingency features of the Mexican 1986–1987 package are also discussed by Cline, MOBILIZING BANK LENDING, at 30–32; and by Hewitt, Adrian P., *Stabex and Commodity Export Compensation Schemes: Prospects for Globalization*, 617–631 WORLD DEVELOPMENT, vol. 15, no. 5, 1987, at 630.

entitled 'New Money Financing for Growth-oriented Adjustment and Structural Reform in Mexico', dated as of March 20, 1987. In addition to the contingency financing facilities, described in the following, the multi-facility agreement contained a symmetry-provision pursuant to which a favorable change of external factors which brought Mexico increased external revenues would trigger a prepayment of advances and a reduction in bank commitments; this mechanism will be discussed later.

The growth-related contingency financing facility

The growth-related portion of the financing, denominated 'Facility 3', was an arrangement for the amount of US $500 million which linked commercial bank disbursement to drawdowns under Mexico's stand-by arrangement with the IMF, which itself contained an 'oil contingency mechanism'.[258]

The IMF Oil Contingency Mechanism is tied in the Multi-Facility Agreement in the form of a communication from the IMF annexed as schedule E.[259] The communication states at the outset that '[the mechanism] is designed to prevent a disruption in the program and in Mexico's balance of payments due to unforeseen changes in oil prices.' The mechanism assumes an average band for the price of oil between $9 and $14 a barrel; as long as the average oil price remained within such band, the arrangement provided there would be no adjustment to Mexico's 'net external borrowing targets'. Variations below the relevant band could trigger contingency financing, as described in the following, whereas surges above the band could entail reduction in bank financing, as described further below.

The triggering event under the commercial bank facility itself was a shortfall in the growth rate of the economy, as measured

---

[258]Commercial bank financing under 'Facility 3' was further linked to the effectiveness of World Bank sectoral loans. The linkage to IMF and World Bank financing was made by incorporating effective disbursement under the IMF facility, and the conclusion of World Bank agreements, in the definition of 'availability dates'; this was spelled out in Section 2.02 of the Agreement.

Commercial bank lending under Facility 3 further benefited from a guarantee given by the IBRD, provided for in under Section 10.01, (c) of the Multi-Facility Agreement.

The World Bank may issue guarantees under the authority of Article III of its Articles of Agreement.

[259]'Communication from the IMF Re IMF Oil Contingency Mechanism', dated February 24, 1987.

by an 'index of manufacturing production' specified in the agreement. The IMF was to act as the agent in charge of certifying that the agreed shortfall had occurred. In addition, since the credit was intended to support growth-generating projects, loans were made conditional upon the identification, by the IBRD and the Mexican Government, of appropriate projects to be financed. The relevant drawdown conditions read:

> The Commitments of Facility 3 (Growth Cofinancing) shall be available to the Borrower subject to the following additional conditions:
>
> (1) The Commitments of Facility 3 (Growth Cofinancing) shall be available only after receipt by the Agent of a certificate of the IMF, in the form of Exhibit 8, which confirms that the conditions for activating Facility 3 (Growth Cofinancing) as described in Schedule D and in such certificate have been met.
>
> (. . .)
>
> (2) Each Borrowing Request for utilization of [Facility 3] shall be effective only when the Agent shall have received a confirmation of IBRD, substantially in the form of Exhibit 9, which confirms that (i) IBRD and Mexico have jointly identified suitable projects for financing under Facility 3, which projects will be described in reasonable detail and assessed as Projects having significant employment generation and substantial spillover effects on the private sector in Mexico; (ii) such Projects are in areas in which IBRD has ongoing programs relating to existing or future IBRD relating to existing or future IBRD loans (. . .) (iii) the disbursement of the amount requested in the Borrowing Request will be entitled to the IBRD Facility 3 Guaranty as provided in Article X.

The triggering event thus was to be formalized by a certificate to be sent to Citibank, NA, as agent bank under the agreement, by the IMF. Exhibit 8 of the Agreement contained a form of such certificate, central to the whole contingent financing operation:

> The International Monetary Fund hereby certifies with respect to Facility 3 (Growth Cofinancing) described in Schedule D to the Agreement that (1) the percentage increase between the first quarter of 1986 and the first quarter of

1987 in the index of manufacturing production (calculated on the basis of the average of the three months in the quarter) is below minus 1.0 percent and (2) the conditions approved by the Executive Board of the Fund for activating Facility 3 (Growth Cofinancing) have been met.

The notion of 'index of manufacturing production', in turn, was described in Schedule D to the Multi-Facility Agreement, which consisted in a communication by the IMF to the commercial banks involved:

The index of manufacturing production is prepared by the Bank of Mexico on the basis of information from a monthly industrial survey carried out by the General Statistical Office, data gathered directly from firms in specific sectors, and information obtained from selected public sector enterprises. This index was chosen as a 'proxy' for the level of output of the Mexican economy because it is available with only a relatively short delay and bears a strong statistical relationship to real GDP.

The contingent investment support facility

The investment support facility, a credit agreement in the total amount of US $1.2 billion, was equally complex in that it linked disbursements to arrangements between the Mexican government, the IMF and World Bank. In addition, it specified drawdown conditions which were the actual 'contingency' portion of the financing.

The triggering event, rather than the shortfall in growth used under Facility 3, was a shortfall in Mexico's public sector external receipts. A direct reference to the price of oil was intentionally avoided.[260] The agent in charge of certifying that the event had materialized was again the International Monetary Fund. The relevant conditions read:

Each Borrowing Request for utilization of Facility 4 (Investment Support) shall be effective only when the Agent shall have received a certificate of the IMF, substantially in

---

[260]This was reportedly due to resistance on the part of lenders. Interview with Washington DC attorney involved in sovereign debt restructuring, September 14, 1990.

the form of Exhibit 10, which confirms that (i) cumulative drawings under the IMF Oil Contingency Mechanism equivalent to at least US $200 million have been made and that an additional amount has been drawn under such Mechanism in respect of the applicable calendar quarter for the requested Borrowing; (ii) based on appropriate consultations with Mexico and the IBRD, the IMF has determined that a shortfall in Mexico's public sector external receipts (both oil and non-oil) has occurred which will reduce Mexico's capacity to maintain its 1986–1987 budgeted public sector investment program and, therefore, the requested Borrowing is necessary in order to help protect the ongoing implementation of Mexico's budgeted public sector investment program. (. . .)[261]

Reduction in commitments

Contingency financing provisions have as their counterpart clauses providing for reduction in lenders' commitment in case of an overall improvement in the financial condition of the borrower, in the form, for instance, of windfall export earnings. In such case, instead of providing additional financing, the external circumstance entails a reduction in outstanding commitment.

To be sure, clauses providing for reduction in creditors' commitments do not address the central problem of this study, which is adaptation of contracts under changed circumstances which are adverse, not favorable, to borrowers. They should nevertheless be viewed as part of a package which would make adaptation provisions which are protective to the interest of borrowers more palatable to lenders.

The Mexican restructuring agreement of 1986–1987 contained one such mechanism.

Mexico 1986–1987

The main features of the agreement were described above, upon discussion of contingency financing mechanisms. The new money facilities – the refinancing portion of the package – were spelled out in a multi-facility agreement named 'New Money

[261]Exhibit 10 essentially repeated the language of the provision reproduced above.

Financing for Growth-oriented Adjustment and Structural Reform in Mexico', dated as of March 20, 1987.

The relevant clause in the agreement provided that incremental revenues, if any, obtained by Mexico as a result of an appreciation in the price of oil would be applied to prepay advances already made, as well as reduce commitments, under the four new money facilities. The determination as to the occurrence of incremental external revenues would be made by the International Monetary Fund, which had itself an oil contingency facility under its stand-by arrangement with Mexico, as mentioned above. The communication stated that 'commercial bank financing to Mexico [would] be reduced under the Upper-end Scenario', which featured the average price of oil rising above $14 a barrel for any given quarter.

The mechanism required determination as to the existence and amount of incremental revenues, to be made by the IMF; calculation of the actual reduction amount, to be made by the Agent, which was Citibank, NA, and application thereof, pursuant to a given priority which was spelled out in the agreement. The relevant provision in the Agreement read:

Section 5.12. *Application of Incremental External Revenues.*
(a) *IMF Certificates and Definitions.* Schedule E sets forth the text of a communication from the Managing Director of the IMF to the Banks describing the IMF Oil Contingency Mechanism. Such Communication states that the IMF Contingency Financing Mechanism applies to five calendar quarters: the last calendar quarter of 1986 and each calendar quarter of 1987. Such Communication also states that the IMF will deliver, within 60 calendar days after the end of each such calendar quarter in 1987, to the Borrower for delivery to the Agent, a certificate of the IMF confirming either the absence or the amount of the incremental external revenues to Mexico during such calendar quarter under the IMF Oil Contingency Mechanism. The Borrower agrees that it will promptly deliver to the Agent each such certificate received by the Borrower from the IMF. For purposes of this Section, the following terms shall have the following meanings:

'*Aggregate Incremental External Revenues*' means, as of any date of determination, an amount in US Dollars equal to the

147

sum of all amounts certified by the IMF as of such date as incremental external revenues to Mexico under the IMF Oil Contingency Mechanism, which certification by the IMF shall be made pursuant to one or more certificates of the IMF substantially in the form of Schedule F.

'*Reduction Amount*' means, as of any date of determination, an amount in US Dollars equal to 75% of the excess, if any, of the Aggregate Incremental External Revenues as of such date, over US $200 million, *less* any portion of the Reduction amount previously applied pursuant to subsection (c) below.

(b) *Calculation of Reduction Amount.* The Agent shall calculate the Reduction Amount, if any, as of the 75th calendar day after the end of each calendar quarter in 1987. Such calculation shall be based solely on certificates of the IMF received by the Agent on or prior to such date as to incremental revenues to Mexico under the IMF Oil Contingency Mechanism. The Agent shall promptly notify the Banks, the Borrower and IBRD of both the Reduction Amount, if any, as of each such date of calculation and the amount, if any, of such Reduction Amount to be applied pursuant to paragraphs (1), (2), (3) and (4) of subsection (c) below. If such application of the Reduction Amount shall require a prepayment under paragraph (1), (3) or (4) of subsection (c) below, the Agent shall calculate the Amount of each prepayment due in each Loan Currency and notify the Borrower, the Banks and IBRD of the Loan Currency, Facility, amount and payment date of each such required prepayment. Each such notification by the Agent shall be conclusive in the absence of manifest error.

(c) *Application of Reduction Amount to Mandatory Prepayment of the Facilities and to Reduction of the Commitments.* The Reduction Amount shall be applied to prepay the Advances under and to reduce the Commitments for the Facilities in the following order:

(1) *first*, to prepay ratably each Facility 4 Advance then outstanding (. . .)

(2) *second*, to reduce the Commitments for Facility 1 (Parallel New Money) and Facility 2 (Cofinancing New Money) (. . .)

(3) *third*, to prepay ratably each Facility 1 Advance and each Facility 2 Advance then outstanding (. . .) and *then*,

(4) *fourth*, to prepay ratably each Facility 3 Advance then outstanding (. . .)[262]

provided that
if the Reduction Amount, as so calculated by the Agent for
any of the first four (but not the fifth) calendar quarters
identified in subsection (a) above, shall be less than US
$50,000,000, the Reduction Amount shall not be so applied
pursuant to paragraphs (1) through (4) above at such time
but shall be carried forward to a subsequent calendar
quarter.

The specifics of the contingency financing facilities included in
the Mexico 1986–1987 package met the particular circumstances
of a global debt restructuring agreement engineered for a major
debtor in the context of a debt crisis, a restructuring which
necessarily involved the multilateral financial institutions. Thus,
bank contingency commitments were linked to IMF and World
Bank financing and were made conditional upon the IMF certifying that certain triggering events had materialized.

Clearly, for contingency financing clauses to become a workable proposition for international development loan agreements,
a more simplified structure would need to be devised, which
does not rely on the international financial institutions. While
these had a central role in the global strategy for handling the
debt crisis of the 1980s, they cannot be expected to intervene
in every single syndicated loan agreement concluded with a
developing country borrower in the context of voluntary, 'fresh'
lending. Expertise to draw such a simplified structure could be
drawn from the value recovery mechanisms described above,
which have moved away from the use of the International Monetary Fund as calculation agent to the appointment of a common
agent of the parties.

With respect to 'downward indexation', the clause under the
'New Money Financing for Growth-oriented Adjustment and
Structural Reform in Mexico' which provides for the reduction
in banks' commitments – as well as to prepayment of advances
already made – constitutes the first precedent in indexation
entailing a reduction in banks' obligations. The new money

---

[262]Each of the items on application specified the amount and date of such application; the amount was determined in relation to the amount of the then
outstanding principal of each facility.

portion restructuring packages usually amounted to involuntary lending designed at filling the restructuring country's financing gap. In that context, in those instances where total disbursements were not made up-front, it was logical for the creditors to want their commitments to be reduced should the debtor country subsequently benefit from an improved balance of payments position.

Chapter Seven

ADAPTATION CLAUSES: A WORKABLE PROPOSITION?

The generalized inclusion of adaptation provisions in transnational financing transactions involving developing country borrowers would amount to a marked departure from standard practice. The discussion of adaptation therefore begs the question as to whether such provisions would be desirable and acceptable to all parties concerned.

As regards borrowers, the benefits of adaptation clauses are clear. Adaptation provisions could significantly reduce their vulnerability to shifting circumstances and directly enhance their ability to fulfill contractual obligations under adverse conditions. Liability management for both private and public sector borrowers in a developing country, as well as for the sovereign itself, would be improved under contractual terms which allowed for cash-flow predictability.

To be sure, the inclusion of adaptation provisions in contractual arrangements would, in all likelihood, entail not only protection against adverse changes in circumstances, but also elimination of potential gains from favorable changes. It is assumed, however, that debt managers would only contemplate and seek adaptation mechanisms when financial calculations demonstrated that the prospect of speculative gains is outweighed by the benefits derived from smoothened and predictable financial obligations. In addition, the framework for the protection against external shocks would ideally be complemented by debtors' resorting to market-based risk-hedging techniques such as the ones discussed in Part I of this study, in connection with which gains resulting from favorable changes could also be assured.

The disruptive experience of the debt crisis of the 1980s, and indeed of earlier crises, would seem to demonstrate that adap-

151

tation of the terms of contractual arrangements in light of dramatically changed circumstances may be required one way or another, due to sheer inability, on the part of borrowers, to fulfill obligations as originally spelled out in the contract. This is particularly true in the case of medium- to long-term obligations. Given such seemingly inexorable need to adapt the terms of the relevant agreements under dramatically changed circumstances, the argument can be made that it would be in the interest of both parties to establish, in the agreements which bind them, the terms under which such adaptation will occur, rather than have it crafted in the context, not devoid of animosity, of debt restructuring exercises once payment difficulties arise.

The argument that the framework for development financing would be sounder, and contractual disruptions less likely, with the widespread adoption of contractual flexibility through adaptation clauses, speaks in favor of the generalized adoption of such mechanisms. However, while such argument is relevant from a policy perspective, it is unlikely, absent concrete motivations, to prompt creditors in the market-place to agree to provisions which depart from established practice and seem detrimental to their interests. The advantages of avoiding the time- and resource-consuming exercise of arm-twisting around negotiation tables designed to put together complex restructuring packages, which characterized the relationship between developing country borrowers and private sector creditors throughout the 1980s, would probably be insufficient motivation for creditors to agree to contractually foreseen adaptation.

As a general proposition, lenders seek certainty regarding income streams. Even in those instances where, for tax reasons or otherwise, creditors view non-accruing assets in a favorable light, there is an understandable preference towards knowing the rules of the game in advance. Any of the adaptation mechanisms envisaged in this study – renegotiation, interest capping, interest capitalization, indexation and even contingency financing and provisions regarding reduction of commitments – would, in principle, run counter to this basic interest creditors have.

Moreover, the market perspective of liability management would in all likelihood indicate market-based instruments as the most suitable way to hedge against risks related to external variables such as fluctuations in interest rates, currency parities and commodity prices. As discussed in Part I of this study, while this strategy is certainly the one most indicated in the case of individual corporate borrowers which have limited liabilities to hedge, it is probably unfeasible in the case of sovereigns managing their external indebtedness. Even in those cases where resort to derivatives is feasible, the optimization of debt management may point to a combination of both strategies – market-based and contractually foreseen adaptation.

The discussion of specific instances and modalities of adaptation provisions, undertaken above, seem to demonstrate that in addition to the general, policy consideration regarding the advantages of contractually foreseen adaptation over *ad hoc* adaptation, specific adaptation provisions may be carefully conceived so as to meet the needs and interests of creditors and debtors alike.

It seems, in light of the precedents of adaptation provisions reviewed above, that *bilateralism* probably lies in the center of the balance to be struck in contractual relationships between debtors and creditors, as regards the matter of adaptation. In other words, adaptation provisions would be most palatable when designed to work both ways: relief to debtors under adverse circumstances – in the form of temporarily reduced interest burden, or additional financing – could be provided for in exchange for corresponding financial benefits for creditors, the most direct translation of which is increased rates of interest in favorable circumstances. A variation of relief to debtors is the agreement on a 'base' rate of interest below market levels, coupled with the right for creditors to benefit from windfall gains, as was the case in the issue of *Participating Notes* by the Argentinian company, as reviewed above.

In any case, the precedents discussed above are clearly in support of the proposition that contractual mechanisms which adequately link borrowers' financial obligations to their capacity to meet them are technically conceivable; and may be acceptable to all parties concerned.

CONCLUSION

Payment difficulties met by developing country borrowers in connection with the developing country debt crisis of the 1980s were aggravated by a combination of adverse changes in external economic circumstances which directly or indirectly impaired their ability to fulfill contractual obligations; a similar phenomenon had occurred in previous generalized crises of external indebtedness.

The legal instrument which evidenced the bulk of developing country external indebtedness at the time the debt crisis of the 1980s erupted was a medium- to long-term floating interest rate loan agreement, often entered into with bank creditors organized under a syndicate. Such instruments did not envisage circumstances under which the relevant obligors were under strain to fulfill payment obligations as a result of circumstances which escaped their control; accordingly, no relief for borrowers was provided for such situations under the terms of the governing instrument. As a result of such contractual rigidity, borrowers and creditors had to renegotiate the terms of their contractual arrangements, in a process which resulted in the conclusion of successive restructuring agreements.

This study has submitted that the legal framework of transnational financing transactions involving developing country borrowers would be more sound if the relevant governing instruments provided borrowers with flexibility in performing payment obligations under adverse circumstances. The study has attempted to discuss, in a systematic manner, the range of provisions into which such flexibility would translate. Provisions regarding the adaptation of borrowers' obligations could conceivably entail interest capping and/or capitalization, or indexation of payment obligations to some measure of the obligors' ability to pay. Conversely, lenders' obligations could be adapted through the provision of contingency financing. There are precedents of all types of clauses discussed in the documentation regarding transnational financing transactions involving developing country borrowers.

The analysis of individual adaptation clauses undertaken in this study has attempted to demonstrate that creditors can derive benefits from them, depending on specific market circumstances and on the manner in which the provision in question is crafted. Such attactiveness of specific features of adaptation provisions adds to a policy concern that recommends the generalization of such adaptation provisions, as an efficient alternative to the hazardous, time- and resource-consuming process of renegotiating debt obligations as and when payment difficulties arise – a traumatic process which characterized the relationship between developing country borrowers and their creditors throughout the 1980s.

From the standpoint of borrowers, the benefits of adaptation provisions are even more evident. Adaptation provisions could significantly reduce their vulnerability to shifting circumstances and directly enhance their ability to fulfill contractual obligations under adverse conditions. Liability management for both private and public sector borrowers in a developing country, as well as for the sovereign itself, would be improved under contractual terms which allowed for cash-flow predictability.

As regards legal technique, mechanisms built into documentation implementing developing country debt restructuring agreements which link payment obligations to some measure of the debtor's capacity to pay, under so-called 'value recovery' or 'recapture' clauses, provide an elaborate illustration of what contractual provisions linking obligation to pay to capacity to pay could resemble. Similar structures were also implemented in the context of voluntary financing to LDC borrowers, which linked obligation to pay interest to the effective performance of the debtor.

Such adaptation mechanisms, as conceived and agreed to date, have only provided for *incremental* payments to be made by developing country borrowers in connection with *favorable* subsequent changes, such as increased export revenues. The agreed provisions demonstrate that there is legal engineering available

155

to build upon in order to achieve a workable two-sided mechanism.

In such a scenario, triggering events would need to be conceived so as to determine an appropriate *deterioration* in a given measure of a country's or corporate borrower's financial condition – such as export revenues, or trade balance or GDP growth in the case of the sovereign – as opposed to an *improvement* in such measures. Suspension, modification and cancellation features, such as the ones adopted in the country restructuring agreements reviewed in this study, could be built into the mechanism, so as to level out cash flow over time and to allow for parties to the transaction to always have a realistic trigger.

Indexed financing would be more easily conceivable in the case of a country which derives most of its hard currency earnings from one single export item, or of a single private sector exporter, although some of the precedents reviewed demonstrate that more general indicators of capacity to pay – such as a basket of commodities and GDP – could also be used as the relevant measure for adaptation provisions. The framework under development financing for the protection of developing country borrowers' transactions against adverse changes in circumstances would ideally be complemented by the generalized use, on the part of such borrowers, of market-based risk-hedging instruments, which should become increasingly accessible to them.

On a final note, it should be said that for adaptation clauses to be written into bond documentation and loan agreements, they must be proposed in the first place. It is up to borrowers and their counsels to raise the issue of adaptation in the course of negotiations of the relevant documentation, for collectively they are the party most interested in such departure from standard practice.

BIBLIOGRAPHY

Sources

Treaties and related documents

Agreement to Amend the Financial Agreement of December 6, 1945, done between the USA and the United Kingdom on March 6, 1957; TIAS 3962.

Article IV, Section 4(c) of the Articles of Agreement of the World Bank, dated December 27, 1945, UNTS 134.

Articles of Agreement of the International Bank for Reconstruction and Development. Entered into force December 27, 1945, 2 UNTS 134.

Articles of Agreement of the International Monetary Fund. Entered into force December 27, 1945, 2 UNTS 39.

Articles of Agreement of the EBRD, entered on May 29, 1990, are reproduced in ICSD REVIEW – FOREIGN INVESTMENT LAW JOURNAL, vol. 5, n. 2, fall 1990, p. 326.

PROCEEDINGS AND DOCUMENTS OF THE UNITED STATES MONETARY AND FINANCIAL CONFERENCE. Bretton Woods, New Hampshire, July 1–22, 1944 (2 volumes, United States Government Printing Office, 1948).

Statutes and subordinate legislation – domestic and regional

(Brazilian) Senate Resolution No. 82/1990, *Diário Oficial*, December 28, 1990.

(Brazilian) Senate Resolution No. 98/1992, *Diário Oficial*, December 29, 1992.

COM (90) 141 final, OJNo. C 152/6 6 (1990) (Document of the Commission of the European Communities).

EC Council Directive (89/645/EEC) of 18 December 1989 on a solvency ratio for credit institutions, OJNo. L 386/14 (89).

International Lending Supervision Act, Pub. L. No. 98–181, 97 Stat. 1153, 1278 (1983) (codified at 12 USCA §§ 3901–3913 (Supp. 1 1983).

12 United States Code of Federal Regulations 208.

157

International organizations – selected documents

IBRD General Conditions Applicable to Loan and Guarantee Agreements. Dated January 1, 1985.

SELECTED DECISIONS AND SELECTED DOCUMENTS OF THE INTERNATIONAL MONETARY FUND, Washington DC, IMF, 16th issue, May 31, 1991.

International organizations – reports and official studies

AID FOR DEVELOPMENT: THE KEY ISSUES. SUPPORTING MATERIALS FOR THE REPORT OF THE TASK FORCE ON CONCESSIONAL FLOWS, Washington DC, IMF/World Bank Development Committee, 1986, 138p.

Compensatory financing of export earnings shortfalls, Report of the Expert Group of the UNCTAD. New York, United Nations, 1985, TD/B/1029/Rev. 1.

DETERMINANTS AND SYSTEMIC CONSEQUENCES OF INTERNATIONAL CAPITAL FLOWS. IMF Occasional Paper no. 77. Washington DC, IMF, March 1991, 94p

Dillon, K. Burke, Duran-Downing, Luis, and Xafa, Miranda, OFFICIALLY SUPPORTED EXPORT CREDITS. DEVELOPMENT AND PROSPECTS. World Economic and Financial Surveys. Washington DC, IMF, February 1988, 47p.

Expanded Cofinancing Operations, World Bank, Cofinancing and Financial Advisory Services, January 1991.

FINANCIAL ORGANIZATION AND OPERATIONS OF THE IMF. (By the Treasurer's Department of the International Monetary Fund). IMF Pamphlet Series no. 45. Washington DC, IMF, 119p., 1990.

Johnson, G.G., Fisher, Matthew, and Harris, Elliott, OFFICIALLY SUPPORTED EXPORT CREDITS. DEVELOPMENT AND PROSPECTS, World Economic and Financial Surveys, Washington DC, IMF May 1990. Appendix IV, p. 38.

IMF *Annual Reports*.

INTERNATIONAL CAPITAL MARKETS, DEVELOPMENTS AND PROSPECTS, IMF World Economic and Financial Surveys. Washington DC, IMF, April 1990.

MANAGING FINANCIAL RISKS IN INDEBTED DEVELOPING COUNTRIES. IMF Occasional Paper no. 65. Washington DC, International Monetary Fund, June 1989, 47p.

OECD *Development Cooperation Reports*.

Pownall, Roger and Stuart, Brian, *The IMF's Compensatory and Contingency Financing Facility,* 9 FINANCE AND DEVELOPMENT, December 1988.

PRIVATE MARKET FINANCING FOR DEVELOPING COUNTRIES, World Economic and Financial Surveys, Washington DC, International Monetary Fund, December 1992, 80p.

RECENT INNOVATIONS IN INTERNATIONAL BANKING, Basle, Bank for International Settlements, April 1986, 270p.

RISK MANAGEMENT GUIDELINES FOR DERIVATIVES, Basle Committee on

Banking Supervision, Bank for International Settlements, July 1994, 19p.

THE EXPORT CREDIT FINANCING SYSTEM IN OECD COUNTRIES, Paris, OECD, 3rd edition, 1987.

TRANSNATIONAL BANKS AND THE EXTERNAL INDEBTEDNESS OF DEVELOPING COUNTRIES. IMPACT OF REGULATORY CHANGES, United Nations Document ST/CTC/SES.A/22. New York, United Nations, 1992, 48p.

World Bank Annual Reports.

International organizations – publications

ASSET AND LIABILITY MANAGEMENT BY BANKS, OECD, Paris 1987, 176p.

Buchheit, Lee C., *Documentation Issues and Alternative Techniques of Debt Restructuring*, 1–28 LATIN AMERICAN SOVEREIGN DEBT MANAGEMENT. LEGAL AND REGULATORY ASPECTS (Ralph Reisner, Emilio J. Cardenas and Antonio Mendes editors), Washington DC, Inter-American Development Bank, 1990, 273p.

Buchheit, Lee C., *Overview of Four Debt Reduction Programs: Mexico, Costa Rica, the Philippines and Venezuela*, 77–86 LATIN AMERICAN SOVEREIGN DEBT MANAGEMENT. LEGAL AND REGULATORY ASPECTS (Ralph Reisner, Emilio J. Cardenas and Antonio Mendes editors), Washington DC, Inter-American Development Bank, 1990, 273p.

Buchheit, Lee C., and Reisner, Ralph, *Inter-Creditor Issues in Debt Restructuring*, 28–51 LATIN AMERICAN SOVEREIGN DEBT MANAGEMENT. LEGAL AND REGULATORY ASPECTS (Ralph Reisner, Emilio J. Cardenas and Antonio Mendes editors), Washington DC, Inter-American Development Bank, 1990, 273p.

Cizauskas, Albert C., *The Changing Nature of Export Credit Finance and its Implications for Developing Countries*, World Bank Working Paper no. 409, Washington DC, World Bank, July 1980, 28p.

CURRENT LEGAL ISSUES AFFECTING CENTRAL BANKS (Robert C. Effros editor), Washington DC, International Monetary Fund, 1992, vol. 1, 642p.

CURRENT LEGAL ISSUES AFFECTING CENTRAL BANKS (Robert C. Effros editor), Washington DC, International Monetary Fund, 1992, vol. 1, 642p.

Davis, Richard J., *Coping with 'Fatigue' in the Debt-Restructuring Process*, 147–153 CURRENT LEGAL ISSUES AFFECTING CENTRAL BANKS (Robert C. Effros editor), Washington DC, International Monetary Fund, 1994, vol. 2, 465p.

EXTERNAL DEBT MANAGEMENT (Hassanali Mehran editor), Washington DC, IMF, 1985, 322p.

Fedder, Marcus J.J., and Mukherjee, Mohua, *The Reemergence of Developing Countries in the International Bond Markets*, 63–119 BEYOND SYNDICATED LOANS. SOURCES OF CREDIT FOR DEVELOPING COUNTRIES (John D. Shilling, editor), World Bank Technical Paper No 163, Washington DC, World Bank, 1992, 119p.

Gold, Joseph, FINANCIAL ASSISTANCE BY THE INTERNATIONAL MONETARY FUND: LAW AND PRACTICE, IMF Pamphlet Series no. 27. Washington DC, IMF, 2nd edition 1980.

Gold, Joseph, LEGAL AND INSTITUTIONAL ASPECTS OF THE INTERNATIONAL MONETARY SYSTEM, Washington DC, International Monetary Fund, 1984.

Gold, Joseph, LEGAL EFFECTS OF FLUCTUATING EXCHANGE RATES, Washington DC, IMF, 1990, 473p.

Gold, Joseph, ORDER IN INTERNATIONAL FINANCE: THE PROMOTION OF STAND-BY ARRANGEMENTS AND THE DRAFTING OF PRIVATE LOAN AGREEMENTS, IMF Brochure no. 39, Washington DC, IMF, 1982.

Gold, Joseph, *Relations Between Bank's Loan Agreements and Fund Stand-by Arrangements*, 781–802 Gold, Joseph, LEGAL AND INSTITUTIONAL ASPECTS OF THE INTERNATIONAL MONETARY SYSTEM, Washington DC, IMF, 1984.

Gold, Joseph, *The Legal Character of the Fund's Stand-by Arrangements and Why it Matters*, IMF Pamphlet Series no. 35. Washington DC, IMF, 1980, 53p.

Goreux, Louis M., CONTINGENCY FINANCING FACILITY, IMF Pamphlet Series no. 34, 1980, 84p.

Hay, Jonathan and Bouchet, Michel H., THE TAX, ACCOUNTING AND REGULATORY TREATMENT OF SOVEREIGN DEBT, Washington DC, World Bank Cofinancing and Financial Advisory Services Department, September 1989, 99p.

Hay, Jonathan and Paul, Nirmaljit, REGULATION AND TAXATION OF COMMERCIAL BANKS DURING THE INTERNATIONAL DEBT CRISIS, World Bank Technical Paper Number 158, World Bank, Washington DC, 1991, 216p.

Kalderen, Lars, *Techniques of External Debt Management*, 99–111 EXTERNAL DEBT MANAGEMENT (Hassanali Mehran editor), Washington DC, IMF, 1985, 322p.

Lamdany, Ruben, *The Market-Based Menu Approach in Action: The 1988 Brazilian Financing Package*, 163–175 DEALING WITH THE DEBT CRISIS (Ishrat Husain and Ishac Diwan editors), World Bank, 1989, 308p.

Masuoka, Toshiya, ASSET AND LIABILITY MANAGEMENT IN THE DEVELOPING COUNTRIES. MODERN FINANCIAL TECHNIQUES, World Bank Working Paper WPS 454, Washington DC, World Bank, 1990, 56p.

O'Brien, Richard R., PRIVATE BANK LENDING TO DEVELOPING COUNTRIES: PAST, PRESENT AND FUTURE, World Bank Staff Working Paper No. 482, Washington DC, World Bank, August 1981, 54p.

Stumpf, Mark H., and Debevoise, Whitney, *Overview of Techniques: Raising New Money, Growth Facilities, Cofinancing and Collateralized Borrowings*, 53–75 LATIN AMERICAN SOVEREIGN DEBT MANAGEMENT. LEGAL AND REGULATORY ASPECTS (Ralph Reisner, Emilio J. Cardenas and Antonio Mendes editors), Washington DC, Inter-American Development Bank, 1990, 273p.

SYSTEMIC RISKS IN SECURITIES MARKETS, Paris, OECD 1991, 64p.

Wallich, Christine I., *The World Bank's Currency Swaps*, FINANCE & DEVELOPMENT, June 1984.

Books

ADAPTATION AND RENEGOTIATION OF CONTRACTS IN INTERNATIONAL TRADE AND FINANCE (Norbert Horn editor), Antwerp, Kluwer, 1985, 421p.

Bergstein, C. Fred, Cline, William R., and Williamson, John, BANK LENDING TO DEVELOPING COUNTRIES: THE POLICY ALTERNATIVES, Washington DC, Institute for International Economics, 1985, 210p.

Borchard, Edwin, and Wynne, WH, STATE INSOLVENCY AND FOREIGN BONDHOLDERS. Vol. I, GENERAL PRINCIPLES, New York, Garland, 1983, 381p.

Boughaba, Mohammed, LES CLAUSES D'ADAPTATION ÉCONOMIQUE ET MONÉTAIRE DANS LES CONTRATS PRIVÉS INTERNATIONAUX, Lausanne, Entlebuch, 1984, 356p.

Cline, William R., INTERNATIONAL DEBT AND THE STABILITY OF THE WORLD ECONOMY, Washington DC, Institute for International Economics, 1983, 134p.

Cline, William R., INTERNATIONAL DEBT: SYSTEMIC RISKS AND POLICY RESPONSES, Washington DC, Institute for International Economics, 1984, 336p.

Cline, William R., MOBILIZING BANK LENDING TO DEVELOPING COUNTRIES, Washington DC, Institute for International Economics, 1987, 92p.

COMMODITY RISK MANAGEMENT AND FINANCE (Theophilos Privolos and Ronald C. Duncan editors), Washington DC, Oxford University Press, 1991.

CORPORATE AND SOVEREIGN BORROWERS IN DIFFICULTY (David Suratgar editor), London, Euromoney, 1984, 163p.

De Covny, Sheree, and Tacchi, Christine, HEDGING STRATEGIES, New York, Woodhead Faulkner, 1991, 202p.

DEFAULT AND RESCHEDULING. CORPORATE AND SOVEREIGN BORROWERS IN DIFFICULTY (David Suratgar editor). London, Euromoney, 1984, 163p.

Delaume, Georges, LEGAL ASPECTS OF INTERNATIONAL LENDING AND INTERNATIONAL FINANCE, New York, Oceana, 1967, 371p.

Delaume, Georges, TRANSNATIONAL CONTRACTS. APPLICABLE LAW and SETTLEMENT OF DISPUTES. (A Study in Conflict Avoidance), New York, Oceana. 5 volumes (loose-leaf publication)

EXCHANGE RATE RISKS IN INTERNATIONAL CONTRACTS, Paris, ICC Institute, 1987, 431p.

FOREIGN DEVELOPMENT LENDING. LEGAL ASPECTS (Seymon J. Rubin editor), Leiden, Sijthoff and New York, Dobbs Ferry, 1971, 352p.

GUIDELINES ON LEGAL NEGOTIATIONS WITH COMMERCIAL LENDERS (Lars Kalderen and Qamar S. Siddiqi editors), London, Butterworths, 1984, 264p.

Hardy, Chandra S., RESCHEDULING DEVELOPING COUNTRY DEBTS, 1956–1981: LESSONS AND RECOMMENDATIONS, Washington DC, Overseas Development Council, June 1982, Monograph no. 15, 74p.

Holmgren, Christina, LA RENÉGOTIATION MULTILATÉRALE DES DETTES PUBLIQUES: LE CLUB DE PARIS AU REGARD DU DROIT INTERNATIONAL; thesis; available as manuscripts at the libraries of the University of Geneva and Graduate Institute of International studies, Geneva.

Horn, Norbert, DAS RECHT DER INTERNATIONALEN ANLEIHEN, Frankfurt, Athenäum, 1972, 572p.

Impallomeni, E.B., IL PRINCIPIO REBUS SIC STANTIBUS NELLA CONVENZIONE DI VIENNA SUL DIRITTO DEI TRATTATI, Milano, Giuffrè, 1974, 54p.

INTERNATIONAL FINANCIAL LAW. LENDING, CAPITAL TRANSFER AND INSTITUTIONS (Robert S. Rendell editor), London, Euromoney, 1980, 304p.

INTERNATIONAL FINANCIAL LAW. LENDING, CAPITAL TRANSFERS AND INSTITUTIONS (Robert S. Rendell editor). London, Euromoney, 2nd edition, 1984.

INTERNATIONAL SECURITIES LAW AND PRACTICE (J. Michael Robinson editor), London, Euromoney, 1985, 303p.

JUDICIAL ENFORCEMENT OF INTERNATIONAL DEBT OBLIGATIONS (David M. Sassoon and Daniel D. Bradlow editors), Washington DC, International Law Institute, 1987, 173p.

LATIN AMERICAN SOVEREIGN DEBT MANAGEMENT. LEGAL AND REGULATORY ASPECTS (Ralph Reisner, Emilio J. Cardenas and Antonio Mendes editors), Washington DC, Inter-American Development Bank, 1990, 273p.

Lessard, Donald R., and Williamson, John, FINANCIAL INTERMEDIATION BEYOND THE DEBT CRISIS, Washington DC, Institute of International Economics, September 1985, 118p.

Lissakers, Karin, BANKS, BORROWERS AND THE ESTABLISHMENT. A REVISIONIST ACCOUNT OF THE INTERNATIONAL DEBT CRISIS, New York, Basic Books, 1991, 308p.

Lomax, David F., THE DEVELOPING COUNTRY DEBT CRISIS, New York, St Martin's Press, 1986, 317p.

Malard, Arielle, LE COFINANCEMENT BANQUE MONDIALE – BANQUES COMMERCIALES, Paris, PUF 1988, 87p.

Mason, Edward S. and Asher, Robert E., THE WORLD BANK SINCE BRETTON WOODS, Washington DC, Brookings Institution, 1979, 915p.

Mosler, Mathias, FINANZIERUNG DURCH DIE WELTBANK. GRUNDLEGUNG UND ANWENDBARES RECHT DER VERTRAGLICHEN INSTRUMENTE, Berlin, Dunckler & Humblot, 1987, 203p.

Mudge, Alfred, Sovereign Debt Restructuring: A Current Perspective, 85–90 DEFAULT AND RESCHEDULING. CORPORATE AND SOVEREIGN BORROWERS IN DIFFICULTY (David Suratgar editor), London, Euromoney, 1984, 163p.

Parker, Cheryl, THE WORLD BANK: A CRITICAL ANALYSIS, New York, Monthly Review Press, 1982, 414p.

Peter, Wolfgang, ARBITRATION AND RENEGOTIATION OF INTERNATIONAL

INVESTMENT AGREEMENTS. A STUDY WITH PARTICULAR REFERENCE TO MEANS OF CONFLICT AVOIDANCE UNDER NATURAL RESOURCES INVESTMENT AGREEMENTS, Dordrecht, Martinus Nijhoff, 1986, 297p.

Peter, Wolfgang, ARBITRATION AND RENEGOTIATION OF INTERNATIONAL INVESTMENT AGREEMENTS. A STUDY WITH PARTICULAR REFERENCE TO MEANS OF CONFLICT AVOIDANCE UNDER NATURAL RESOURCES INVESTMENT AGREEMENTS, 2nd edition, revised and enlarged. The Hague; Boston: Kluwer Law International, 1995, 458p.

Petersmann, Hans G., FINANCIAL ASSISTANCE TO DEVELOPING COUNTRIES: THE CHANGING ROLE OF THE WORLD BANK AND THE INTERNATIONAL MONETARY FUND. INSTITUTIONAL, LEGAL AND POLICY PERSPECTIVES, Bonn, Forschungsinstitut der Deutschen Gesellschaft für Auswärtige Politik e.V., 1988, 123p.

Schmithoff, Clive M., EXPORT TRADE, THE LAW AND PRACTICE OF INTERNATIONAL TRADE, London, Stevens & Sons, 9th edition 1990, 798p., p. 190.

Shihata, Ibrahim, THE EUROPEAN BANK FOR RECONSTRUCTION AND DEVELOPMENT. A COMPARATIVE ANALYSIS OF THE CONSTITUENT AGREEMENT, London/Dordrecht/Boston, Martinus Nijhoff, 1990, 189p.

Shihata, Ibrahim, THE WORLD BANK IN A CHANGING WORLD. SELECTED ESSAYS, Dordrecht, Martinus Nijhoff, 1991, 490p.

Sinclair, Ian, THE VIENNA CONVENTION ON THE LAW OF TREATIES, Manchester, University Press, 2nd edition, 1984, 270p.

SOVEREIGN BORROWERS. GUIDELINES ON LEGAL NEGOTIATIONS WITH COMMERCIAL LENDERS (Lars Kalderen and Qamar S. Siddiqi editors), London, Butterworths, 1984, 264p.

THE COLLECTED WRITINGS OF JOHN MAYNARD KEYNES. VOL. 25, ACTIVITIES 1940–1944: SHAPING THE POST-WAR WORLD: THE CLEARING UNION (D. Moggridge editor), 1990. (Collection in the Joint Library of the IMF/World Bank in Washington DC.)

The Outlook for International Bank Lending (M.S. Mendelsohn editor), Washington DC, Group of Thirty, 1981, 51p.

Williamson, John, VOLUNTARY APPROACHES TO DEBT RELIEF, Washington DC, Institute for International Economics, 1989, 66p.

Wood, Philip, LAW AND PRACTICE OF INTERNATIONAL FINANCE, London, Sweet & Maxwell, 1980, 462p.

Wood, Philip, LAW AND PRACTICE OF INTERNATIONAL FINANCE, Volume 2A. International Business & Law Series, New York, Clark Boardman Co., Ltd., 1990.

Articles

Abi-Saab, Georges, Le Droit au développement, 9–24 ANNUAIRE SUISSE DE DROIT INTERNATIONAL XLIV (1988).

Adede, A.O., Legal Trends in International Lending and Investment in the Developing Countries, 9–168 RCADI 1983–II.

Allsopp, Christopher, and Joshi, Vilai, The Assessment – The International

Debt Crisis, i–xxxiii OXFORD REVIEW ECONOMIC POLICY vol. 2, n. 1, 1986.

Asser, Tobias M.C., *The World Bank and the Renegotiation and Adaptation of Long-Term Loans*, 253–269 ADAPTATION AND RENEGOTIATION OF CONTRACTS IN INTERNATIONAL TRADE AND FINANCE (Norbert Horn editor), Antwerp, Kluwer, 1985, 421p.

Baumann, Martin F., and Harvey, Jr., Richard J., *LDC Debt Strategies: Accounting and Tax Issues*, 198–217 LATIN AMERICAN SOVEREIGN DEBT MANAGEMENT. LEGAL AND REGULATORY ASPECTS (Ralph Reisner, Emilio J. Cardenas and Antonio Mendes editors), Washington DC, Inter-American Development Bank, 1990, 273p.

Bhandari, Jagdeep S., *International Debt Litigation in United States Courts*, 383–421 GERMAN YEARBOOK OF INTERNATIONAL LAW, vol. 33 (1990).

Brady, Nicholas D., *Statement*, 69–76 THIRD WORLD DEBT: THE NEXT PHASE (Edward R. Fried and Philip H. Trezise editors), Washington DC, The Brookings Institution, 1989, 118p. (*Report of a Conference held in Washington DC, on March 10, 1989*).

Brainard, Lawrence J., *Emerging Market Sovereign Debt. A New Evaluation Framework*, New York, Goldman Sachs, Emerging Debt Markets Research. October 4, 1991, 21p.

Broches, Aron, *The World Bank*, 83–96, 2 INTERNATIONAL FINANCIAL LAW. LENDING, CAPITAL TRANSFERS AND INSTITUTIONS (Robert S. Rendell editor), London, Euromoney, 2nd edition 1984.

Broches, Aron, *International Legal Aspects of the Operations of the World Bank*, RCADI 1959-III, 297–409

Buxbaum, Richard, *Modification and Adaptation: American Developments*, 31–54 ADAPTATION AND RENEGOTIATION OF CONTRACTS IN INTERNATIONAL TRADE AND FINANCE (Norbert Horn editor), Antwerp, Kluwer, 1985, 421p.

Camdessus, Michel, *Government Creditors and the Role of the Paris Club*, 125–130 Default and Rescheduling: Corporate and Sovereign Borrowers (David Suratgar editor), London, Euromoney, 1984, 163p.

Carreau, Dominique, *Le Rééchelonnement de la dette extérieure des Etats*, 5–48 JOURNAL DU DROIT INTERNATIONAL 1985.

Crozer, George K., and Wall, Duane D., *The Eurodollar Market: Loans and Bonds*, 63–78 INTERNATIONAL FINANCIAL LAW. LENDING, CAPITAL TRANSFER AND INSTITUTIONS (Robert S. Rendell editor), London, Euromoney 2nd edn 1984, 200p.

Dooley, Michael P., and Watson, C. Maxwell, *Reinvigorating the Debt Strategy*, 8–11 FINANCE & DEVELOPMENT, September 1989, p. 8.

Edwards, Richard W., *Is an IMF Stand-by Arrangement a 'Seal of Approval' on which other Creditors can Rely?* 573–597 NEW YORK UNIVERSITY JOURNAL OF INTERNATIONAL LAW AND POLITICS vol. 17 (1985).

Eichengreen, Barry, and Portes, Richard, *The Anatomy of Financial Crises*, 10–58 THREATS TO INTERNATIONAL FINANCIAL STABILITY (Richard Porter and Alexander K. Swoboda editors), Cambridge, Cambridge University Press, 1987, 307p.

El-Erian, Mohamed A., *Mexico's Commercial Bank Financing Package*, 26–27 FINANCE & DEVELOPMENT September 1990.

Fishlow, Albert, *Lessons from the Past: Capital Markets during the 19th Century and the Interwar Period*, 383–439 INTERNATIONAL ORGANIZATION vol. 39, n. 3, (1985).

Fouchard, Philippe, *Adaptation of Contracts to the Economic Climate*, 6–73/ 6–89 ARBITRATION AND THE LICENSING PROCESS (Robert Goldscheider and Michel de Haas, editors), New York, Clark Boardman Co., Ltd., 1984.

Frenkel, Orit, and Fontheim, Claude G.B., *Export Credits: An International and Domestic Legal Analysis*, 1069–1088 LAW & POLICY IN INTERNATIONAL BUSINESS vol. 13 (1981).

Gianviti, François, *The International Monetary Fund and External Debt*, 209–286 RCADI 1989 III

Gold, Joseph, *Natural Disasters and Other Emergencies Beyond Control: Assistance by the IMF*, 621–641 THE INTERNATIONAL LAWYER, fall 1990.

Griffith-Jones, Stephany, *Ways Forward from the Debt Crisis*, 39–61 OXFORD REVIEW ECONOMIC POLICY vol. 2, n. 1 (1986).

Gruson, Michael, and Feuring, Wolfgang, *The New Banking Law of the European Community*, 1–40 THE INTERNATIONAL LAWYER vol. 25 (1991).

Harvey, Charles, *On Reducing the Risk in Foreign Finance – for Both Parties*, Institute for Development Studies Discussion Paper no. 167, November 1981, 160p.

Helleiner, G.K., *Relief and Reform in Third World Debt*, 113–124 World Development (1979).

Hewitt, Adrian P., *Stabex and Commodity Export Compensation Schemes: Prospects for Globalization*, 617–631 WORLD DEVELOPMENT, vol. 15, no. 5, 1987.

Higgins, Sovereign Lending and IMF Conditionality, IFLR May 1984.

Horn, Norbert, *Changes in Circumstances and the Revision of Contracts in some European Laws and in International Law*, 15–29 ADAPTATION AND RENEGOTIATION OF CONTRACTS IN INTERNATIONAL TRADE AND FINANCE (Norbert Horn editor), Antwerp, Kluwer, 1985, 421p.

Horn, Norbert, *Standard Clauses on Contract Adaptation in International Commerce*, 111–140 ADAPTATION AND RENEGOTIATION OF CONTRACTS IN INTERNATIONAL TRADE AND FINANCE (Norbert Horn editor), Antwerp, Kluwer, 1985, 421p.

Hudes, Karen, *Coordination of Paris and London Club Reschedulings*, 553–571 NEW YORK UNIVERSITY JOURNAL OF INTERNATIONAL LAW AND POLITICS vol. 17 (1985).

Hurlock, James B., *Legal Implications of Interest Rate Caps on Loans to Sovereign Borrowers*, 543–552 NEW YORK JOURNAL OF INTERNATIONAL LAW AND POLITICS vol. 17 (1985).

Knieper, Rolf, *The Conditioning of National Policy-Making by International Law: The Standby Arrangements of the International Monetary Fund*, 41–64 INTERNATIONAL JOURNAL OF THE SOCIOLOGY OF LAW no. 11 (1983).

Kuczynski, Pedro-Pablo, *Latin American Debt*, 344–364 FOREIGN AFFAIRS, winter 1982/1983.

Lichtenstein, Cynthia C., *The US Response to the International Debt Crisis: the International Lending Supervision Act of 1983*, 401–434 VIRGINIA JOURNAL OF INTERNATIONAL LAW (1985).

Lichtenstein, Cynthia C., *Introductory Note*, 27 ILM 524 (1988), 524–527.

Logan, Francis D., *Term Loan Agreements*, 11–23 INTERNATIONAL FINANCIAL LAW. LENDING, CAPITAL TRANSFER AND INSTITUTIONS (Robert S. Rendell editor), London, Euromoney, 1980, 304p.

Logan, Francis D., and Rowntree, Peter D., *Term Loan Agreements*, 1–14 I INTERNATIONAL FINANCIAL LAW. LENDING, CAPITAL TRANSFER AND INSTITUTIONS (Robert S. Rendell editor), London, Euromoney, 1983, 200p.

Mann, F.A., *The Proper Law of Contracts Concluded by International Persons*, 34 THE BRITISH YEARBOOK OF INTERNATIONAL LAW 1959.

Martha, Rutsel Silvester J., *Preferred Creditor Status under International Law: the Case of the International Monetary Fund*, 801–826 ICLQ vol. 39 (1990).

Morais, Herbert V., *World Bank Promotion of Private Investment Flows to Developing Countries through Cofinancing and other Measures*, 1–37 ICSID REVIEW – FOREIGN INVESTMENT LAW JOURNAL spring 1988.

Mudge, Alfred, *Sovereign Debt Restructure: A Perspective of Counsel to Agent Banks, Bank Advisory Groups and Servicing Banks*, 59–74 COLUMBIA JOURNAL OF TRANSNATIONAL LAW vol. 23 (1984).

Mudge, Alfred, *Country Debt Restructure, 1982–87: An Overview*, 141–146 CURRENT LEGAL ISSUES AFFECTING CENTRAL BANKS (Robert C. Effros editor), Washington DC, International Monetary Fund, 1992, vol. 1, 642p.

Norton, Joseph Jude, *The Multidimensions of the Convergence Processes Regarding Prudential Supervision of the International Banking Acts – The Impact of the Basle Supervisors' Committee Efforts Upon, Within and Without the EC*, 249–324 FESTSCHRIFT JOSEPH GOLD, Heidelberg, Recht und Wirtschaft, 1990, 470p.

Nurick, Lester, *Negotiation of Transnational Bank Loan Agreements Entered into by Developing Country Borrowers: Legal and other Issues*, 43–79 ISSUES IN NEGOTIATING INTERNATIONAL LOAN AGREEMENTS WITH TRANSNATIONAL BANKS, New York, United Nations Centre on Transnational Corporations, 1983; ST/CTC/48, 103p.

Oppetit, Bruno, *L'Adaptation des contrats internationaux aux changements de circonstances: la clause de 'hardship'*, 794–814 JOURNAL DU DROIT INTERNATIONAL (1974).

Peter, Wolfgang, *Adaptation and Renegotiation Clauses*, 29–46 JOURNAL OF INTERNATIONAL ARBITRATION vol. 3, n. 2 (1986).

Privolos, Theophilos, *Experience with Commodity-Linked Issues*, 11–38 COMMODITY RISK MANAGEMENT AND FINANCE (Theophilos Privolos and Ronald C. Duncan editors), Washington DC, Oxford University Press, 1991.

Rieffel, Alexis, *The Paris Club, 1978–1983*, 83–110 COLUMBIA JOURNAL OF TRANSNATIONAL LAW vol. 23 (1984).

Quale, Jr., Andrew C., *New Approaches to LDC Debt Reduction and Disposition: US Legal and Accounting Considerations*, 605–627 THE INTERNATIONAL LAWYER vol. 23 (1989).

Rieffel, Alexis, *The Role of the Paris Club in Managing Debt Problems*,

Essays in International Finance no. 161. Princeton, Princeton University, December 1985, 38p.

Roberts, Steven M., *Capital Adequacy and LDC Debt: The Impact of the Basle Agreement*, TRENDS AND FORCES IN INTERNATIONAL BANKING LAW Seminar, Bern 26–30 March 1990, 15p., processed

Schmithoff, Clive M., *Hardship and Intervener Clauses*, 415–423 CLIVE M. SCHMITHOFF'S SELECT ESSAYS ON INTERNATIONAL TRADE LAW (Chia-Jui Cheng editor), Dordrecht, M. Nijoff 1988.

Semkow, Brian W., *Syndicating and Rescheduling International Financial Transactions: A Survey of the Legal Issues Encountered by Commercial Banks*, 869–927 INTERNATIONAL LAWYER, vol. 18, n. 4, fall 1984.

Shihata, Ibrahim, *The Role of the European Bank for Reconstruction and Development in the Promotion and Financing of Investment in Central and Eastern Europe: A Legal Analysis*, 207–231 ICSID REVIEW – FOREIGN INVESTMENT LAW JOURNAL vol. 5, fall 1990.

Silard, Stephen, *International Law and the Conditions for Order in International Finance: Lessons of the Debt Crisis*, 963–976 THE INTERNATIONAL LAWYER vol. 23, winter 1989.

Smith, Carsten, and Follak, K.P., *The New Capital Standards of International Banks: Support or Obstacle to Development Aid and External Debt Management?* Paper included in the report of the Committee on International Monetary Law of the International Law Association at the 1990 Conference (Australia), 14p., processed.

Stockmayer, Albrecht, *Excluding Project Loans from Sovereign Reschedulings*, IFLR March 1985

Taylor, John L., *A Lawyer's View of Developments in World Bank Cofinancing with Private Banks*, 415–448 CURRENT ISSUES OF INTERNATIONAL FINANCIAL LAW (David Pierce, Helena Chan, Frederick Lacroix and Philip Pillai editors), published on behalf of the Faculty of Law, National University of Singapore by Malaya Law Review and Butterworths 1985.

The Outlook for International Bank Lending (M.S. Mendelsohn editor), Washington DC, Group of Thirty 1981, 51p.

Tigert, Ricki Rhodamer, *Regulatory Perspectives on Debt-for-Equity Swaps and Securitization of Loans to Heavily Indebted Countries*, 186–197 LATIN AMERICAN SOVEREIGN DEBT MANAGEMENT. LEGAL AND REGULATORY ASPECTS (Ralph Reisner, Emilio J. Cardenas and Antonio Mendes editors), Washington DC, Inter-American Development Bank, 1990, 273p.

Ullman, Harold, *Enforcement of Hardship Clauses in the French and American Legal Systems*, 81–106 CALIFORNIA WESTERN INTERNATIONAL LAW JOURNAL vol. 19 (1988).

van Dunné, Jan M., *Adaptation by Renegotiation – Contractual and Judicial Revision of Contracts in Cases of Hardship*, 413–439 THE COMPLEX LONG-TERM CONTRACT. STRUCTURES AND INTERNATIONAL ARBITRATION (Fritz Nicklisch editor), Heidelberg, C.F. Müller, 1987, 597p.

van Ommeslaghe, Pierre, *Les Clauses de force majeure et d'imprévision (Hardship) dans les contrats internationaux*, 7–59 REVUE DE DROIT INTERNATIONAL ET DE DROIT COMPARÉ (1980).

Venkatachari, K., *The Eurocurrency Loan: Role and Content of the Contract*, 73–122 SOVEREIGN BORROWERS. GUIDELINES ON LEGAL NEGOTIATIONS WITH COMMERCIAL LENDERS (Lars Kalderen and Qamar S. Siddiqi editors), London, Butterworths, 1984, 264p.

Walde, Thomas, *The Sanctity of Debt and Insolvent Countries: Defenses of Debtors in International Loan Agreements*, 119–145 JUDICIAL ENFORCEMENT OF INTERNATIONAL DEBT OBLIGATIONS (David M. Sassoon and Daniel D. Bradlow editors), Washington DC, International Law Institute, 1987, 173p.

Walker, Mark A., and Buchheit, Lee C., *Legal Issues in the Restructuring of Commercial Bank Loans to Sovereign Borrowers*, 459–474 INTERNATIONAL BORROWING. NEGOTIATING AND STRUCTURING INTERNATIONAL DEBT TRANSACTIONS (Daniel D. Bradlow editor), Washington DC, International Law Institute, 2nd edition 1986, 499p.

Wickersham, Warren G., *Problems of Documentation in Rescheduling of Sovereign Bank Debt*, 117–123 DEFAULT AND RESCHEDULING. CORPORATE AND SOVEREIGN BORROWERS IN DIFFICULTY (David Suratgar editor), London, Euromoney, 1984, 163p.

Williamson, John, *The Outlook for Debt Relief or Repudiation in Latin America*, 1–6 OXFORD REVIEW ECONOMIC POLICY, vol. 2, n. 1 (1986).

Wilson, Nicholas, *Bond Issue Documentation*, 190–199 SOVEREIGN BORROWERS. GUIDELINES ON LEGAL NEGOTIATIONS WITH COMMERCIAL LENDERS (Lars Kalderen and Qamar S. Siddiqi editors), London, Butterworths, 1984.

Wood, Philip, *Debt Priorities in Sovereign Insolvency*, 4–11 IFLR November 1982.

INDEX